The subject of apostleshi
eration for today's chu
and refreshing perspecti

Among the books on contemporary apostolic leadership I think Mike Breen's is one of the best. He allows the New Testament to speak for itself so that we might have a fuller understanding of apostolic ministry. He also embodies many of these characteristics in his own ministry in Sheffield and far beyond. He represents a new generation of leadership which I believe will be used of God to bring renewal to the church and a fresh impetus to its mission in the world.

Eddie Gibbs, Professor of Church Growth, Fuller Theological Seminary

This book gives a fresh perspective on the basics of apostolic ministry starting with the ministry of Jesus. Of particular interest is that it outlines a practical way in which every believer can participate in apostolic ministry and thus completely avoids the elitism which so commonly afflicts discussion of the apostolic. For that reason it is well worth reading and thinking about.

Steve Nicholson, Senior Pastor, Evanston Vineyard, and National Leader of the Vineyard Church Planting Team

'Apostle' means different things to different people. This notebook is important, instructive and inspiring.

Sandy Millar, Rector, Holy Trinity Brompton

For those of us who believe that the church will change more in the next 20 years than it has in the last 250, Mike Breen's book is a 'must-read'. God has not only given him a pastor's heart, but he's given him a sharp, a very sharp, mind. Both are seen in abundance in these pages. Any church leader who wants to put their finger on the pulse of this new era had better start right in this book. Whether you agree with his answers or not, he certainly asks the right questions.

Gordon MacDonald, bestselling author and international speaker

The Apostle's Notebook

MIKE BREEN

Series Editor: Barry Kissell

KINGSWAY PUBLICATIONS
EASTBOURNE

ISBN 1 84291 007 8

Published by
KINGSWAY COMMUNICATIONS LTD
Lottbridge Drove, Eastbourne BN23 6NT, England.
Email: books@kingsway.co.uk

Book design and production for the publishers by
Bookprint Creative Services, P.O. Box 827, BN21 3YJ, England.
Printed in Great Britain

In memory of Kathleen Breen,
my pioneering mother – gone to find a new frontier.

Acknowledgements

I would like to acknowledge all those leaders, mentors and friends who have revealed the ministry of Christ to me. I would like to thank the members of St Thomas Church Sheffield for their help and encouragement, and particularly Paul Richards for his work on the Ministries Questionnaire in Chapter 7. I would like to thank my Staff Team for all of their many kinds of help, and particularly Arlene Moore for her help in the preparation of this manuscript. Special thanks, of course, goes to my family and my dear wife, Sally, who knows more about the subject of this book than I ever will!

Contents

Introduction to the Series

With many of my contemporaries, I have had the incredible privilege of being involved in three significant moves of the Holy Spirit.

As a student in the 1960s, studying theology mostly from an academic point of view, I could hardly believe it when, sitting in the college library one day revising for an examination, I started spontaneously to speak in tongues. Shortly afterwards I had an extraordinary revelation during which I heard the voice of God. The charismatic movement within the churches was such a great blessing to those who entered into it. This visitation of the Spirit transformed the life of the church in which I served and all the churches that welcomed his coming.

In the late 1970s I knew that there was going to come a new movement of the Spirit. I had heard the Lord say that it would be known as the 'Third Wave'. In our family this wave struck my wife Mary first. John Wimber prayed for her at a meeting in our church. She returned home on fire. The fire radiated from her for at least twenty-four hours. Its outworking has been seen in significant teaching, healing and counselling gifts. This has been equally true for the many others who were empowered in those days. If the charismatic movement was the rediscovery of the living Jesus and the gifts of his Spirit, then the Third Wave involved meeting with the anointed Jesus and the power of the Holy Spirit.

In the early 1990s a significant move of the Spirit happened in Toronto, Canada, and spread to other nations. Six months previously, on a hillside outside Shepton Mallet in Somerset, the Lord had shown me a vision in which I saw water flowing in every conceivable form. As I watched in wonder, he told me that he was going to refresh his church. What I subsequently saw happening was the Lord delivering people from bondages which had imprisoned them for years, even lifetimes. After the deliverance came a refreshing and incredible joy.

During three decades I have been based at one church and have experienced these moves of the Spirit within the same congregation. From St Andrew's, Chorleywood, I have travelled with Faith Sharing teams to over a thousand churches in twenty-three nations and have watched similar manifestations of the Spirit according to the particular season.

Over these years I have been in both large and small gatherings. I have seen the power of God falling upon countless numbers of people, anointing them to minister in God's church as apostles, prophets, evangelists, pastors and teachers. On many occasions I have heard the Lord ask me this same question: 'I have anointed them, but where are the mature?' By now these minis-tries should be active in all congregations of Spirit-filled churches.

During these different moves of God I have kept notebooks in which I jotted down what I believed to be significant revelations of God to me. These have included visions, dreams and words. It was from these notebooks that the idea for this series was born. Most of the authors would not claim to be theologians. Their expertise, if any, has been in taking note of truths from God which have helped them in developing their min-istries as apostles, prophets, evangelists, pastors and teachers.

I sense that this present 'lull' of the Spirit is in its later stages. The next wave of the Spirit is already building significantly and will soon be breaking upon the churches. There will be fire in the cities and a great ingathering of people to the churches.

It is important that we take God's anointing and calling seriously. We need to be committed to seeking maturity in God's gifting on our lives. In the coming days all five of these ministries will be crucial in the equipping and leading of the churches. We pray that the insights of this series will encourage you on your way to maturity and fruitfulness in the kingdom of God.

Barry Kissell

Preface

Writing this book has been one of the most interesting and difficult experiences I've yet encountered. When I was asked to write something on apostolic ministry, I felt as though someone was asking me to describe my own nose – I knew it was there, I just didn't know how to write about it !

After some preliminaries about the culture and our mission context, the book seeks to explore apostolic ministry using Jesus as the starting point. He is the apostle and high priest of our calling, and as such was the first 'sent one'. I am convinced that the world needs more people who recognize that they are 'sent' by God to bring his kingdom, share his gospel and build his church. Being 'sent' means being part of God's apostolic mission – part of his desire to reach a lost world.

Of course at some point we have to study Ephesians 4. My own interpretation of this text is thought by some to be quite different. But I believe that what I present here both reflects scriptural truth and releases many into areas of Christian ministry that have been inaccessible up until now.

My hope is that all Christians, whether lay or ordained, whether functioning inside the organized church or outside it, whether leading in the workplace or the home, will find help in this short book.

1

Apostolic Mission to the Emerging Culture

Apostolos (Greek NT): One sent as a messenger or agent, the bearer of a commission, messenger, an apostle.[1]

When I was ordained in 1983, I cannot remember anyone even mentioning the possibility of present-day apostolic ministry. How things have changed! Today we find that there is open discussion of apostolic ministry within traditional mainstream Christianity. Through the growth of the Pentecostal and charismatic movements, what was once the province of small interest groups has begun to influence all of evangelical Christianity worldwide.

Recently I surveyed the material available on apostolic ministry, and I was surprised to discover just how much there was. Books and other publications are multiplying: interest is increasing. A quick look at the Christian press reveals conferences that confidently advertise the presence of apostles on the speaking teams. Articles in Christian magazines, tapes, training

---

[1] *Analytical Greek Lexicon* (Samuel Bagster & Sons Ltd, 1973), p. 47.

courses and all the plethora of the Christian resource industry seem to be focused on the apostolic right now.

When I reflect on this, two questions emerge in my mind. Why all the interest? And what is an apostle anyway? Taking the second question first, an apostle is (as we can see from the definition above) one who is sent out. Jesus specifically and deliberately called his first disciples 'apostles'.

> Jesus went up on a mountainside and called to him those he wanted, and they came to him. He appointed twelve – designating them apostles – that they might be with him and that he might send them out to preach and to have authority to drive out demons. (Mark 3:13–15)

Jesus' intention was to send his apostles (literally his 'sent-out ones') on a mission. The mission was to continue the task that he had taken to himself of making disciples for the kingdom of God. Nonetheless, Jesus calling disciples to follow him, and designating the first to be 'apostles', does not mean that the apostolic ministry is necessarily present today. Jesus made it clear that the twelve disciples had a special role of leadership within the kingdom (see Matthew 19:28). The apostolic teaching is also clearly complete: we no longer need apostles to establish the framework of biblical truth and write it down in the New Testament.

Surely, however, the apostolic ministry of being 'sent out' to continue the mission of Jesus in making disciples for the kingdom has not finished, and so therefore requires a continuation of this special work. Later on we will look at this in more detail, but first we need to return to my two questions. Why all the interest? And what is an apostle anyway?

Having begun to deal with 'what', we ought to look at 'why' – why is it that there seems to be a desire emerging within the world church for an understanding of the apostolic? The simplest answer is that all of this is happening due to a sovereign work of God. Even if we grant this, however, we still need a fuller explanation. Surveying the material available seems to produce three answers:

1. The 'end-time' harvest requires 'end-time' apostles.
2. A restored church – based on New Testament models and values – requires a restored fivefold ministry, including apostles.
3. The rapid and accelerating cultural change that we see all around us demands a fresh impetus in mission that only apostolic ministry can provide.

Looking in more detail, we discover that each of these three explanations for the growth in apostolic ministry comes with a fairly complete theological outlook, and often a denominational or post-denominational setting that supports the assertions.

1. The 'end-time' harvest requires 'end-time' apostles

'End time' has come to be used as a shorthand reference for the study of the events that immediately precede the return of Christ. A group of highly influential writers, teachers and preachers have examined the teaching and preaching of Jesus and that of the whole Bible, especially the book of Revelation, to learn how the church might be best equipped to prepare for the Second Coming.

Personally, I am unconvinced of the arguments that suggest we are in the final harvest before the return of Christ, but there is much within this teaching to challenge us. For instance, those who focus on the 'end times' scenario recognize that for the first time in human history the possibility of reaching every people group on earth is within our grasp in the next few years. Jesus himself said that he would not return until the gospel was preached in every nation (literally among every people group). There are thought to be fewer than 500 unreached people groups in the world, and so the assertion is made that we are presently in the 'end times', and Jesus stands on the threshold of heaven ready to re-enter human history, rapturing his church and ushering in the tribulation and millennial reign of God.

Of course, all Christians desire the return of Christ and if we can hasten his return (see 2 Peter 3:12) we should make every effort to do so. Obviously, effort in our own strength is pointless; we need the empowering of God. The ministries and gifts of the Holy Spirit are sent for this very purpose. The so-called 'fivefold' ministries of apostle, prophet, evangelist, pastor and teacher are particularly important. All these ministries have a special role: the prophet to hear the word of God and interpret the signs of the times; the evangelist to proclaim the gospel; the pastor to care for God's people; the teacher to instruct the church in biblical truth. As pioneering leaders in the mission of Jesus to the world, however, apostles are said to be particularly needed within this end-time harvest as leaders of God's people, providing direction and definition in the task. Some have gone so far as to suggest that such a harvest is only possible with a fresh release of apostolic ministry and power in the church.

2. A restored church requires a restored fivefold ministry, including apostles

The second reason often offered to explain the rise of apostolic ministry is that with the decline of Christendom (i.e. organized and established Christianity) in the West, God is rebuilding his church. With decline comes the opportunity of a fresh start, and so the claim is made that God is returning the church to New Testament models of ministry and mission. One of the reasons offered as to why Christianity in the West has declined is that there has been a dislocation from, and even denial of, the fivefold ministries. Everyone knows what a pastor is, but what about the other four? Everyone has heard of bishops, priests and deacons, but how do they fit within a model of the fivefold ministries?

It is contended that we have drifted so far from the biblical norms of leadership and ministry that the best we can do is to return to what appears to be a simple New Testament framework, and to seek the re-establishment of the first forms of Christian leadership. This would mean a fresh release of biblical ministries and gifts. The rise of Pentecostalism in the twentieth century and the emergence of the charismatic movement have been particularly influential in the establishment of this point of view. As the Holy Spirit has been poured out upon these movements he has distributed his gifts, empowered his people and anointed many individuals to fulfil their God-given destiny as an apostle, prophet, evangelist, pastor or teacher. Such an outpouring has been seen by many within these movements as an authentication of them and a signal of God's intention to restore his church to its scriptural pattern.

3. Accelerating cultural change demands a fresh impetus in mission

The third reason, favoured among academics and missiologists (those who study the nature and purpose of mission), is that the world is going through seismic cultural change. The reason that the word 'seismic' is often used is that it feels as though there has been an earthquake within our culture. All our reference points have changed; our familiar social landscape is now so altered that many find it difficult to navigate a course through life.

The situation reminds me of all those 1970s disaster movies – *Towering Inferno*, *Earthquake*, *The Poseidon Adventure* – where the storyline follows the same basic plot. A sudden and catastrophic event occurs which leaves a group of people trying to find a way to safety. Some are so traumatized by the event that they are unable to help either themselves or others. Many seek individualistic and selfish solutions to a corporate problem, but the ones who succeed are those who form a team – a basic community – to solve the overwhelming difficulties. Not only is such a disaster scenario an accurate illustration of what has happened throughout our society, but it is also a good attempt at offering a solution.

Interestingly, the more recent versions of these catastrophe movies, produced in the last years of the twentieth century and reflecting what some have called 'pre-millennial tension' – e.g. *Deep Impact* and *Armageddon* – have a quite different plot. Now it appears that doomed humanity relies on the intervention of a selfless messianic figure to sacrifice himself for the preservation of humankind.

In the 1970s – soon after the rapid change in our culture began – there appears to be hope that if we pull together, we will survive. By the 1990s – when the scale and speed of change was out of control – we have come closer to the recognition that only the intervention of a Saviour will help. Whether these films are consciously portraying the underlying anxiety of our society or not, what is certain is that they reflect a world that is changing very rapidly and one we have not yet come to terms with. It will be interesting to see how the media respond to the social consequences of the 11th September 2001 and whether the terrorist attacks on the World Trade Center reveal an even greater sense of angst within our social landscape.

The global change seen most clearly in the West has resulted in a post-industrial, high-tech society and a whole new way of thinking, which in the last few years has come to be described as postmodernism. This is an attempt to make sense of a world with no familiar reference points (like the victims in the disaster movies). We are trying to understand a world that no longer submits to the powers of familiar reason and logic. This profoundly affects the way we communicate and, because of this, the way we form community. With the emergence of this new worldview, a whole new context for doing mission has emerged.

Much has been written in recent years which covers in detail the first two reasons I have given for this phenomenon of apostolic ministry – i.e. the end-time harvest and the restoration of the church. The third area, sudden cultural change, has not had a great deal of air time. It may be helpful therefore to look at it a little more closely.

Sudden cultural change

The events of the 11th September 2001 in New York have so imprinted themselves on our memories that it is difficult to bring to mind any disasters before this date, and yet, as I write this chapter, the harrowing and disturbing pictures from the Indian earthquake in Gujarat fill my mind. Tens of thousands of people wandering dazed and homeless. Thousands of homes and buildings rendered to rubble. A landscape and society suddenly and catastrophically changed. The earthquake, thought to be one of the strongest in India's history, lasted less than a minute. It was unexpected, unforeseen, and yet the change that this seismic movement brought was fundamental for all those who lived through its aftermath. I can still see the face of a middle-aged man with his wife and family picking through the debris of their home, trying to salvage whatever they could, saying over and over, 'Everything has gone. We've lost everything.' What was most disturbing was that the man was smiling as he pronounced this tragedy, lost in the unreality and numbness of his grief.

These powerful and disturbing images speak eloquently of the tragedy of the Gujarati earthquake, but also illustrate well the kind of change that is taking place within our world. Such images, for those of us living in the West, have until recently largely been drawn from the disasters that we have seen reported from other parts of the world. Since the 11th September 2001, however, the reality and gravity of such awful events have been brought home to us in a way that no one could have anticipated. It is as though the chaos of accelerating change has finally caught up with even the most insulated and protected of societies, so that now we all feel the weight of the looming catastrophe.

Few recognized the pressures building up within Western civilization as secularization and rationalism reached their fullest expression in the creation of the 'modern West'. Few prophets heralded the degree and extent of change that would take place as these pressures finally found their yield point in the 1960s. A combination of affluence, education and the emergence of mass communication meant that the ideas of the elite intelligentsia became the language of the street. What was once the subject of academic speculation became the content of everyday language. This was most clearly evident in the influence of the booming music industry. People would sing along to John Lennon's 'Imagine' without realizing that they were echoing the thoughts of a generation of radical postmodern thinkers. It would perhaps take another book to describe all these pressures and the yield point. What is certain, however, is that after the 1960s everything changed.

The phenomenal rate of change at the social and political levels of society has been breathtaking and appears to be accelerating. Never before has a society become so permissive, so dislocated and disjointed, so incapable of maintaining order, stability and balance. No one could have expected the emergence of a media- and music-dominated generation. Nor could anyone have foreseen politicians being elected by such small electorates and with such small margins (the majority of Western populations are completely uninterested in the electoral process, it would appear).

People began to think differently, act differently, live differently. Along with this social upheaval, amazing technological advances began to gather momentum. In the 1960s no one owned a personal computer; today wristwatches and microwaves have a greater computer capacity than the mainframes of fifty years ago. Few in the world have been able to keep pace with the rate of technological change. Scientists and engineers continuously produce one new innovation after another.

Certainly, the church in the West was not ready for these changes. The mainstream denominational leaders of today look more like earthquake victims – people in the first stages of grief, stunned and denying reality – than leaders of God's people. Yet as Western civilization and Western Christendom, both so closely related, are shaken to their core, something all at once new and exciting, dramatic and dangerous, is beginning to emerge. This sounds so much like the earthquake mentioned in Hebrews 12, that I cannot fail to mention it.

> At that time his voice shook the earth, but now he has promised, 'Once more I will shake not only the earth but also the heavens.' The words 'once more' indicate the removing of what can be shaken – that is, created things – so that what cannot be shaken may remain. (Hebrews 12:26–7)

God appears to be shaking everything so that what is unshakable – his kingdom – is seen by all. The 'shaking' has produced a great opportunity for the church. To respond adequately, it needs the passion, power and perspective of the New Testament era. It requires a new kind of leadership – apostolic leadership – which can be used by God as a channel for a fresh release of his mission through the church to the world. It is because of this that the sovereign hand of God is causing the church to look again at the fivefold ministries, and particularly the apostolic (see Ephesians 4:11–12).

Perhaps the most exciting response to all of this is what has been called 'the New Apostolic Reformation'.

The New Apostolic Reformation

This is a remarkable movement within the world church, gaining momentum all the time. This movement, seen in various forms, is producing networks and associations committed to evangelism and the establishing of healthy, growing churches often overseen by an apostolic figure or team. The best-known examples that come to mind are the Calvary Chapel network, the Vineyard association of churches, New Frontiers International and Pioneer. Each of these was founded, and in many cases is still overseen, by an apostolic figure who, with a commitment to church-planting, has seen the establishment of a network of many and in some cases thousands of churches.

It appears to be an entirely new phenomenon within recent church history, emerging in the 1970s, flourishing in the 1980s and finding acceptance and academic interest in the 1990s. As a movement, it has been identified by the likes of C. Peter Wagner,[2] Donald E. Miller[3] and Eddie Gibbs,[4] and has been described as the most significant new church phenomenon of recent years.

Many of the apostolic networks are based in Western countries, particularly the USA. They are generally post-denominational in character – i.e. they have come out of mainstream denominations, or define themselves in distinction to these denominations – and are, more often than not, both evangelical and charismatic in style and spirituality. In his recent book, C. Peter Wagner asserts that these new apostolic churches are 'at least as radical as those of the Protestant Reformation almost five hundred years ago', and that they 'constitute the fastest growing segment of Christianity' in virtually every region of the world today.[5]

As decline has gripped the church in Europe, the networks of the New Apostolic Reformation have had

---

[2] C. Peter Wagner, *The New Apostolic Churches* (Regal Books, 1998).

[3] Donald E. Miller, *Reinventing American Protestantism* (University of California Press, 1999).

[4] Prof. Eddie Gibbs, 'Church Growth & Urban Ministry: developing a twenty-first-century church with integration and integrity', January 2001.

[5] C. Peter Wagner, *op. cit.*, p. 19.

increasing influence. Interestingly, church attendance figures in the USA have remained fairly constant over the last fifty years. This has been due to the growth of Pentecostal and charismatic groups which are now giving birth to the new streams and networks of the New Apostolic Reformation. It is not, however, restricted simply to these new groups: it is now beginning to emerge even within mainstream denominations as an enormously important vehicle for church growth and health and for the re-establishment and validation of apostolic ministry.

The apostolic missionary challenge

No serious-minded Christian can avoid discussion or debate about apostolic ministry. Quite clearly, God is up to something! He is allowing the decline of mainstream Christianity to follow the social and cultural changes in the West, while at the same time birthing a new church movement committed to apostolic mission. The challenge of this mission should be focused on the generation born from the 1960s onwards, who will form the majority of the world's population in twenty years' time and who have largely left mainstream Christianity, yet seem to be the most socially aware and spiritually minded generation for decades.

For the church to ready itself for this great new missionary enterprise, we not only need to recognize the opportunities of the future but also the obstacles of the past. Perhaps the church's greatest obstacle has been its tendency to turn in on itself, spending its resources to bring comfort and succour to those already 'in', and largely ignoring those outside. Archbishop William Temple's memorable definition of what a church should be comes to mind: 'The Christian church is the one organism in the world that exists purely for the benefit of its non-members.'[6]

Someone sent me this parable that they found on the Internet. It illustrates very well what is, more often than not, the reality.

The Little Life-Saving Station

On a dangerous sea coast where shipwrecks often occur there was once a crude little life-saving station. The building was just a hut, and there was only one boat, but the few devoted members kept a constant watch over the sea, and with no thought for themselves went out day and night searching for the lost. Many lives were saved by this wonderful little station, so that it became famous. Some of those who were saved, and various others in the surrounding area, wanted to become associated with the station and give their time and money and effort for the support of its work. New boats were bought and new crews trained. The little life-saving station grew.

Some of the members of the life-saving station were unhappy that the building was so crude and poorly equipped. They felt that a more comfortable place should be provided as the first refuge for those rescued from the sea. So they replaced the emergency stretchers with beds and put better furniture in the enlarged building. Now the life-saving station became a popular gathering place (because they used

---

[6] Tony Castle (ed.), *The Hodder Book of Christian Quotations* (Hodder & Stoughton, 1982), p. 36.

it as a sort of club). Fewer members were now interested in going to sea on life-saving missions so they hired professional full-time lifeboat crews to do this work. The life-saving motif still prevailed in this club's emblem.

About this time a large ship was wrecked off the coast, and the hired crew brought in boatloads of cold, wet and half-drowned people. The beautiful new club was in chaos. So the Property Committee immediately had a shower house built outside the club where victims of the shipwrecks could be cleaned before coming inside.

At the next meeting there was a split in the club membership. Many of the members wanted to slow down the club's life-saving activities because they were difficult and a hindrance to the normal interaction and social life of the club. Some members insisted upon life-saving as their primary purpose and pointed out that they were still called a life-saving station. But they were finally voted down and told that if they wanted to save lives of all the various kinds of people who were shipwrecked in these waters, they could begin their own life-saving station down the coast. This they did.

As the years went by, the new station experienced the same changes that had occurred in the old. It evolved into a social club, and yet another life-saving station was founded. History continued to repeat itself, and if you visit the sea coast today you will find a number of exclusive clubs along the shore. Shipwrecks are frequent in these waters, but most of the people drown.

It is amazing how we in the church justify our selfishness and how quickly we overlook the imperative to reach out and save the lost. The only certain consequence of such a life strategy is inevitable decline. Such has been the experience of the mainline denominations in postmodern Europe and the USA. We are getting smaller and older by the minute. In a recent paper, Professor Eddie Gibbs made a similar point. We need to move, he said,

> from being evangelical churches to becoming evangelizing churches, from evangelism as a hiccup in the life of the church to evangelism as the heartbeat in the life of the church . . . The style of evangelism in a post-modern environment is very different from that in a modern environment.[7]

When we look at the adult membership of the church in the West, we find that in general there are three generations present in the church today. Sociologists and church-growth experts disagree on the finer points of classification, but for the sake of simplicity, the way I like to describe them is as follows:

1. The Builders (those over 60 years of age)
2. The Baby Boomers (40–60 years)
3. The Baby Busters (20–40 years)

The leadership, wealth and power of the church is found in the first two groups. The smallest group by far are the Baby Busters, often described as Generation X (or simply Xers). This is true both for mainline denominations and, to a lesser extent, for the new emerging networks and affiliations. This youngest generation most markedly reflects the rapid social change that has taken place. They are most definitely postmodern, post-industrial and 'urban' in their outlook.

---

[7] Gibbs, 'Church Growth & Urban Ministry'.

Understanding Generation X has always been a problem for the rest of us!

One of the best self-portraits I have seen is found in the *Blair Witch Project*. This highly controversial film wonderfully illustrates Xers' values, awareness, weaknesses, strengths, expectations and fears. In the film, a group of Xers, functioning as friends rather than family or colleagues, take on a project to produce a film documentary of the Blair Witch story, which tells of a woodland witch kidnapping and killing children like Hansel and Gretel in the fairytale. The team enter the woods, video-recording as they explore: like so many of their generation, they are better at recording their experiences than interpreting them. They are able to experience but not understand. The collective anxiety of their culture emerges as they discover that they are surrounded by a malevolent force, out to get them – the Blair Witch. Trapped in a world they do not understand, they fall prey to forces they cannot control.

Having spent twenty years working with this age group, this is the best expression of the corporate personality of the generation that I have yet seen. As a generation they have grown up with increasing affluence, greater opportunities for education, and a universal experience of breakdown in marriage and social structures, so that today there is a general experience of anxiety and an apathy towards institutions like government and church, which seem to offer no answers to the questions they ask.

They are individualistic. They recognize no absolute truths, few moral structures. They often come across as cynical, soulless, disaffected, marginalized and lonely, and because of this the other generations find them rebellious, thoughtless, uninterested and incredibly difficult to communicate with. Even those who have been brought up in stable, strong families show many of the characteristics of their generation; like passive smokers, they have 'breathed in' an atmosphere that they themselves may not consciously have created. It is amazing how many good Christian families seem to be producing classic examples of Generation X, even though the children have suffered few of the problems of their society as a whole. They have 'breathed in' a new culture.

If we look briefly at the contemporary context and how to reach it, we discover that there are some exciting and challenging opportunities that the emerging culture presents. We will deal with communication of the gospel in the Reflections section at the end of this chapter, and with the planting of Christian community in Chapter 4.

The social and cultural changes that have produced this emerging generation present the church with the most important challenge to mission for at least 500 years. It is for this reason that we must look again at the methods of mission and the models of ministry present within the church. To do this effectively and credibly, we have to recognize that apostolic ministry (the ministry that leads the church in mission) is not only a must for today's church, but a vital part in our understanding of our culture and society and what we must do to reach it with the gospel of Christ.

Apostolic mission will define not only the models and

methods of Christian ministry, but also how to present the message. Because of our new cultural context, we will need pioneers in gospel communication – those who can engage with the strengths and weaknesses of postmodern thought and find ways into our society's 'collective mind'. For instance, even the most casual glance at the emerging culture reveals that belonging, especially as it is expressed in friendship, has become extremely important for those currently entering adult life. Friendship seems to have replaced family as the single most important social component, and is now presented within the media as the 'glue' that holds the stressed-out individuals of our society together.

When I was a child, *The Generation Game* was the prime-time, must-see TV programme on a Saturday night. On the programme, different generations of the same family competed in various ways against another family for the opportunity of winning the big prize – the chance to memorize as many prizes going past on the conveyor belt as possible. Today the same game has been repackaged and presented as *Friends Like Us*: not families but groups of friends competing for the same big prize.

When I was growing up, we all made sure that we caught the next episode of *The Waltons* and *The Little House on the Prairie* – both idealized presentations of rural family life. Today, programmes like *Friends* and *Ally McBeal* top the viewing figures, and these portray an unrealistic urban lifestyle among angst-ridden Xers struggling with much humour to find security in a big and rather scary world. TV programming in this case reflects a major shift in our culture and in the expectations of young people looking for intimacy and belonging.

In this final section, we will look at the issues more closely, and seek to use them to help us communicate with the emerging culture.

Reflections

Communicating the gospel to the emerging culture

The emerging culture is quite different from anything we have seen before, and if we are to communicate the gospel effectively within this context we have to do the hard work of cultural investigation. We should not fear contamination as we seek to understand the world in which we live, but should see it rather as the most important task to be taken on by any who want to communicate effectively. Once we understand, we can more easily identify with our hearers. Once we identify, we can more effectively shape our presentation of truth, so that we do not surrender what is most important in our message and yet find ways to enable our audience to engage with what we are saying.[8]

Below you will find a model that enables us to take a known value of the emerging culture with which we are seeking to engage and from there develop a method of communication.[9]

---

[8] See David Burnett, *Clash of Worlds* (MARC, 1990).

[9] Mike Breen, *Outside In* (Scripture Union, 1993).

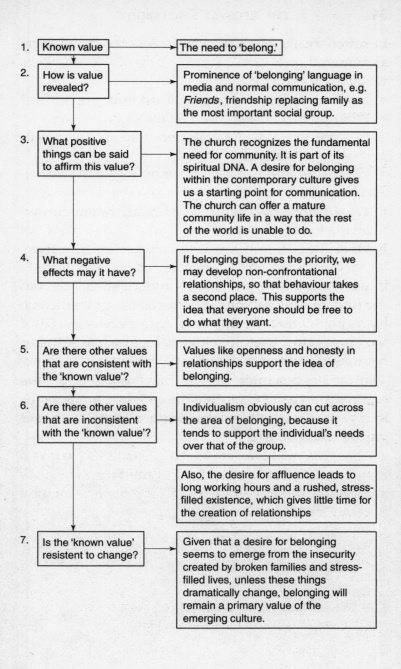

1. | Known value | → | The need to 'belong.' |

2. How is value revealed? → Prominence of 'belonging' language in media and normal communication, e.g. *Friends*, friendship replacing family as the most important social group.

3. What positive things can be said to affirm this value? → The church recognizes the fundamental need for community. It is part of its spiritual DNA. A desire for belonging within the contemporary culture gives us a starting point for communication. The church can offer a mature community life in a way that the rest of the world is unable to do.

4. What negative effects may it have? → If belonging becomes the priority, we may develop non-confrontational relationships, so that behaviour takes a second place. This supports the idea that everyone should be free to do what they want.

5. Are there other values that are consistent with the 'known value'? → Values like openness and honesty in relationships support the idea of belonging.

6. Are there other values that are inconsistent with the 'known value'? → Individualism obviously can cut across the area of belonging, because it tends to support the individual's needs over that of the group.

Also, the desire for affluence leads to long working hours and a rushed, stress-filled existence, which gives little time for the creation of relationships

7. Is the 'known value' resistent to change? → Given that a desire for belonging seems to emerge from the insecurity created by broken families and stress-filled lives, unless these things dramatically change, belonging will remain a primary value of the emerging culture.

In summary, the kinds of questions we need to ask are as follows.

- Is there anything we need to learn from the culture?
- What problems are caused by the inconsistencies?
- In what ways does the culture attempt to answer those inconsistencies?
- What, if anything, does the community of the church have to offer?
- What fears, crises or social pathologies are created by the value?
- How does the message of the cross relate directly?

If we follow this process of investigation, we can develop an effective presentation of the gospel to the emerging culture. In this way, we can be assured of 'holding on to the truth' with one hand while reaching out to the world with the other.

In the next chapter we will move on to begin the exciting journey of exploring the apostolic ministry for today, starting with an examination of the first and greatest of all apostles.

2

Jesus, the Apostle

Now this is eternal life: that they may know you, the only true God, and Jesus Christ, whom you have sent. (John 17:3)

Jesus and the disciples were finishing dinner. They had just celebrated the Passover together. The meal had begun with Jesus embarrassing the disciples by washing their feet, and had continued with him taking the familiar elements of bread and wine and speaking of them in a new way. For the disciples this must have been a confusing and anxious time: many opposed Jesus, and the way that he was talking seemed to indicate that change was in the air. Jesus was saying something about leaving and sending somebody else to take over his role. What did he mean? Why would he leave? Was he unhappy with them? Had they done something wrong? We can all imagine the conflicting thoughts that were rushing through their minds. Jesus, however, seemed confident and offered words of comfort. He told them not to be troubled or afraid. He was leaving his peace with them. Even though he was going away, he promised that he would come back again. Then he stood up from the table and said, 'Come now; let us leave' (John 14:31).

They were out on the streets. They had walked from the upper room, across the flat roof, down the steps and into the thronging streets of Jerusalem. Hundreds of thousands would swell the population at times like this. People would be coming and going all over the city, some having finished their meal, others waiting to start. With their senses arrested by a city alive with celebration, Jesus and his disciples made their way through the streets towards their usual campsite on the Mount of Olives (see Luke 21:37; 22:39). Hearing the Psalms being recited in every home; with the smell of wood smoke, freshly baked bread and roast lamb filling the air; with the sight of doorposts daubed in blood, and homes filled with people and light – they encountered the Passover at every turn.

To get to the Mount of Olives, they needed to go through the Kidron Valley and this almost certainly required a journey past Temple Mount. Walking, Jesus continued to talk over the noise of the city. They approached the west side of the Temple, its white marbled edifice picked out in the light of a myriad oil lamps. And there, glinting, fashioned in gold and set into the stone of the Holy Place, was the symbol of Israel taken from Psalm 80 and found on the coins of an earlier period – a vine.

'I am the true vine and my Father is the gardener . . . you are the branches,' Jesus said as he continued on his way (John 15:1, 5). He went on to explain this picture of spiritual life and fruitfulness. He expected them to produce lots of fruit – living lives that would please the Father.

They walked down the hill, past the cleansing and bathing area on the south side of the Temple where in seven weeks' time 3,000 people would be baptized on the Day of Pentecost. They came to the Kidron Valley, facing the Mount of Olives. Here the prophets said the Messiah would return to open the gates of glory. Here Jesus would bow a bloodied brow and agonize over the decision to go to the cross. Here he would be betrayed by a friend, arrested and taken for trial.

Jesus, his mind filled with conflicting visions of death and glory, imminent pain and future fulfilment, pauses, looks up to the star-filled heavens, and prays. His heart is pulled in many different directions all at once – towards the distant future, towards his disciples listening as he prays, towards a trial, a cross, and a cold tomb. But this stretching, this tension, this pressure also drew him towards his underlying confidence – he was returning to his Father. As he thinks of his return, his heart is stirred to focus on the reason for which he was sent. We listen in with the disciples as we arrive at one of the most holy places in Scripture, one that reveals the intimate relationship between Father and Son. 'Father, the time has come. Glorify your Son, that your Son may glorify you' (John 17:1).

Almost every phrase of this awesome and wondrous prayer arises from and reveals the fundamental understanding in the mind of Jesus about the nature of his mission. He had been 'sent' from the Father (see John 17:3, 18). He uses the word 'sent' (*apostolos*) six times, meaning that he was a person who had been authorized, commissioned and sent with a special task and that he was sending others with the same task.

Jesus the apostle

> It was he who gave some to be apostles, some to be prophets, some to be evangelists, and some to be pastors and teachers, to prepare God's people for works of service, so that the body of Christ may be built up. (Ephesians 4:11–12)

Jesus is the source and embodiment of all five of the ministries listed in Ephesians 4. As such, he defines the terms by which we understand each of them. If we want to know how to be an evangelist (literally 'a bearer of good news'), we look at Jesus: he was the first to come declaring the good news. If we want to know how to be a pastor (literally 'a shepherd' of God's people), again we look to him: he was the Good Shepherd. Likewise, if we want to understand apostolic ministry, we look to the original 'sent one': 'Therefore, holy brothers, who share in the heavenly calling, fix your thoughts on Jesus, the apostle and high priest whom we confess' (Hebrews 3:1).

By his life, Jesus defined each of the ministries, and it is for this reason that when we look at his life as 'the apostle', we begin to discern an apostolic perspective in all that he did, and we also begin to see the Gospels in a new light. They become a handbook of apostolic ministry.

Why have we not seen this before? We have not seen it because our desire to understand apostolic ministry has not been a pressing concern. Most of the church has believed that apostolic ministry died out after the first century AD, and so has found the study of a contemporary application of the apostolic both unnecessary and irrelevant. Centuries have been spent on describing, defining and applying the more familiar ministries. Principally we have wanted to understand pastoral leadership and also, to a lesser extent, the ministries of teaching and evangelism. Could it be that a focus on these 'safer' sides of Jesus' ministry has pauperized our understanding of him and prevented us from seeing a broader picture of Christian leadership?

Interestingly, our artistic representation of Jesus in paintings, stained glass, music and poetry seems to support this idea. Most of the images, except those of his crucifixion, are unmistakably pastoral. The kindly man with cherub-like features carrying the lamb or talking to children is not quite the image of the prophet cleansing the Temple, or the apostle pushing out the frontiers of the kingdom. There have, of course, been artists who have attempted other portrayals of Christ, but the overriding presentation found in our art and supported in our worship and music is a somewhat gentle, non-confrontational Jesus.

Seeing Jesus from a new perspective

Recent church movements have forced us to look afresh at the New Testament, to redefine what we mean by Christian ministry in general and apostolic ministry in particular. If we assume that Jesus is the original apostle, then we can track and interpret his life from a new standpoint. A friend of mine told me of a recent visit to the Sistine Chapel in Rome. Having visited some years before, he was interested to see the results of the restoration of Michelangelo's famous painting on the ceiling. What he found astonished him. He told me that it was as though he had never really seen the painting before. The smoke from thousands of candles and the accumulated grime of the centuries had now been cleaned away. He told me that the average person would see 50 per cent more in the painting and that an expert could see up to 75 per cent more. We can have the same experience when reading the Scriptures from a fresh perspective. It is as though different vistas open on a familiar story. Hidden hues and colours emerge in a picture we thought we knew well. We see features in the landscape of Jesus' life that we had not seen before. And of course this means that we have fresh interpretive keys put into our hands to open old treasures.

We should start with the words of Jesus himself. Jesus described his life and work in particular ways:

From the days of John the Baptist until now, the kingdom of heaven has been forcefully advancing, and forceful men lay hold of it. (Matthew 11:12)

The one who sowed the good seed is the Son of Man. (Matthew 13:37)

For the Son of Man came to seek and to save what was lost. (Luke 19:10)

. . . I will build my church, and the gates of Hades will not overcome it. (Matthew 16:18b)

In other words:

- He came to advance the frontiers of the kingdom forcefully.
- He came to establish a new community.
- He came to rescue the outsiders.
- He came to develop the structures of a new corporate life for God's people.

We can express these tasks as 'pioneering', 'planting', 'bridging' and 'building' – activities which, as we shall see in later chapters, are fundamental to apostolic ministry. When we look at each of these activities, we begin to see Jesus' life from an apostolic perspective, and his ministry as the pattern for the apostles of the New Testament and early church.

Pioneering

The time had arrived. Jesus knew that the moment had come for him to step from the shadows of obscurity into the light of public ministry. He walked into Capernaum declaring war, intending to extend the frontiers of the kingdom of God in the domain of human hearts. His declaration of war was simple: 'It's time. The kingdom of God is here. Change your lives from the inside out and live as if you're included in the good news of God's plan' (see Mark 1:15).

Jesus was looking for a breakthrough in the lives of those who listened. He was looking for ways to push out the boundaries of God's rule expressed in his own life so that it began to touch the lives of others. 'Come, follow me,' he said to the fishermen (Mark 1:17). They followed and, although apparently insignificant, the territory of the kingdom of heaven was now larger – not by much, but still larger.

There was an early response to this incursion by the opposition: the kingdom of light cannot be extended without some kind of response from the kingdom of darkness. As Jesus was in full flow, preaching his first sermon at the synagogue in Capernaum, the enemy stepped in and tried to steal his thunder. 'What do you want with us, Jesus of Nazareth? Have you come to destroy us? I know who you are – the Holy One of God!' (Mark 1:24).

It is one thing to have the apparent charisma to influence people; it is another thing entirely to have the power to defeat a demon. I am sure the atmosphere was charged in that hot and sweaty meeting house. I am sure there was a crackle in the atmosphere as people waited on the response. With stern authority, Jesus said, 'Be quiet . . . Come out of him!' (Mark 1:25). The authority and power resident within Jesus funnelled down into one captive individual. Pressing in with full force on the agent of darkness holding and feeding on the life of the demonized man, the two kingdoms were clashing and crashing into each other. Shaking violently, the man became the battlefield, but the outcome was assured as soon as Jesus spoke: with a shriek, the demon left the man.

As they watched the man being set free, the awe-struck crowd questioned what they were experiencing. Certainly Jesus had won a hearing. It seemed as though the whole town followed him back to where he was staying. He was establishing the house of Peter and Andrew as his headquarters, the centre of his operations. He would return here again and again; it would be a place where many amazing and miraculous things would occur. In Capernaum, Jesus the pioneer was looking first of all for a breakthrough, and then for a bridgehead from where he could continue his work. That's what pioneers do.

In summary, we can say that Jesus the apostle pioneered by:

- claiming lives as new territory for the kingdom of God;
- proclaiming the gospel to any who would hear;
- acting decisively with enemy counterattacks;
- operating in divine authority and power;
- establishing a bridgehead from which he could work.

Planting

Planting and pioneering overlap. Jesus had got the green light from heaven to get on with his long-awaited task. Now he had to establish a new community that would carry forward the purpose of the kingdom of heaven. Communities are made up of people. Jesus had to spot the people who could help him start the process. So, sensitive to the prompting of the Spirit, and watchful of what his Father was doing, Jesus began. One day, when he was walking beside the River Jordan, John the Baptist (who was not too far away) shouted, 'Look, the Lamb of God!' Two of John's disciples decided to investigate (see John 1:35–7). One was Andrew, and the other was probably John. They rather coyly asked Jesus where he was going, and Jesus encouraged them to 'come along and see'. They spent the day with Jesus, and two things happened. First, Andrew became convinced that he had found the Messiah, and Jesus was convinced that he had found the first of many disciples. Second, taking the opportunity that Andrew's friendship afforded, Jesus focused next on his brother Peter and then the other men who were all called to make a commitment to follow him.

Although the crowds increased and his popularity grew, later on in Capernaum Jesus prioritized these relationships and gave more time to his disciples than to anyone else. Jesus was not so much concerned for popularity as he was in planting a new community. Within three years this new 'planting' would be ready to grow and bear fruit. The strategy was a good one: by the time we see the church in the Acts of the Apostles, it has become a self-sustaining, self-propagating community of faith.

As an apostolic planter, Jesus:

- recognized the right time to plant;
- identified the people who could open doors to other relationships;
- prioritized relationship over popularity;
- focused his energy and gifts into a small, gathered group;
- imparted a pattern of community life that could grow and multiply all by itself.

Bridging

To be an apostle, Jesus needed to be able to function in different environments and cultures. As the model apostle, he provides the basic framework for how apostolic cross-cultural ministry can be conducted. For instance, as a communicator Jesus used different models when speaking to the crowds in Galilee and the people in Jerusalem. In general terms, he appears to have used a more narrative approach with the unlettered crowds in Galilee – simple people who could understand stories, pictures and parables (see Mark 4:33). In Jerusalem, by contrast, he uses a more propositional and theological approach, engaging in learned debates with the scribes and Pharisees, and refuting the arguments of clever but spiritually dead theologians (see Mark 12:13–17).

His cross-cultural abilities did not end there. Jesus established an opportunity for the evangelization of the Samaritan people by bridging effectively into the life of one Samaritan woman. There had been contact with other Samaritans, of course, not least the leper whom he healed (see Luke 17:15–16). Yet his conversation with the woman at the well seemed to provide opportunities for him to speak to a whole town and draw the attention of the disciples to a ripening harvest. As the people of Sychar came out to see the man whom the woman claimed was a prophet, Jesus said, 'Open your eyes and look at the fields! They are ripe for harvest' (John 4:35). We are told that many believed in him after his short stay – but many more would believe when the apostles returned to support the work of Philip the evangelist some years later (see Acts 8:14–15).

As an apostolic bridger, Jesus:

- recognized the different needs of different cultures;
- communicated appropriately according to cultural needs;
- used his pioneering and planting gifts to establish a cross-cultural bridgehead;
- addressed cultural prejudices among his disciples so that their eyes would be opened to the new bridging opportunity.

Building

Jesus clearly wanted to establish some basic structures that could be quickly and easily replicated in the movement that would emerge after his death and resurrection. Teamwork was one of these: Jesus established a pattern of using teams wherever possible. He rarely sent individuals – at a minimum he would use a pair. He sent pairs of disciples on mission. He took three up the Mount of Transfiguration. Even for simple tasks, he used a team, sending two to fetch him a donkey (see Mark 6:7; 9:2; 11:1–2).

In such fashion, he established the pattern for the life of the early church, where worship, fellowship and mission were done in community. He established the lightweight structures of a common life and shared purse, which allowed him and his disciples to focus on the tasks of the kingdom without being burdened with the details of administration. These principles were carried forward into the life of the Jerusalem church, which only needed to establish formal administrative structures after growing to several thousand members (see Acts 6:1ff).

Jesus laid down simple, memorable, repeatable teaching which would provide the framework of reality for the early church. He even provided simple strategies of mission (which we will look at in later chapters) which could be used by others in a variety of different contexts. Jesus developed a lightweight, low-maintenance structure for the life of the early church, which allowed it to work with astonishing effectiveness once it was empowered by the Spirit from heaven.

As an apostolic builder, Jesus provided basic structures for the emerging community life of the church, including:

- teamwork;
- shared life;
- common resources;
- repeatable teaching;
- strategies for mission.

Jesus the apostle was the model pioneer, planter, bridger and builder and, as such, cut a path on which we continue to walk to this day. Even for Jesus, however, there was a time of preparation. He lived in obscurity for most of his life, watching, waiting and learning how best to speak and act. Along with this general preparation, there was the specific preparation of the impartation of the Holy Spirit and the testing of his call. All these contributed to releasing the authority and power that Jesus needed to do the work.

Preparation

John had been gathering crowds for some time now. His sermons were powerful and provoking. The people loved it when he corrected the rich and religious. Surely he was a prophet.

Jesus was standing in line, waiting his turn to be baptized, his sense of anticipation growing. He knew that something extraordinary was going to happen. Finally it was his turn. John looked up, hands still wet from the last baptism, eyes as piercing as ever. 'I can't baptize you,' he said. 'You should baptize me.' Without really knowing it, John's prophetic credentials were underlined. He could 'see' that Jesus was no ordinary man. John knew in his heart that before him stood the long-awaited Messiah, the one whose way he had prepared in the wilderness. The King was among them – surely *he* should be the one baptizing.

Jesus said, 'It is right that you baptize me.' He could not ask others to do something he had not already done himself (see Matthew 3:14–15). Without discussion, John understood what Jesus meant. He apprehended a greater purpose and so conceded to Jesus' request. Lowering Jesus below the water was in many ways a routine event – something John had done thousands of times – but at another level it was unique. He had never baptized anyone like Jesus before, and knew that he never would again.

Coming up out of the water, Jesus lifted his eyes

JESUS, THE APOSTLE 51

towards the heavens, where a strange sight began to unfold. There, for all to see, the sky was being torn apart, ripped open, so that those who looked could see past the physical realm to the world beyond (see Mark 1:10). From this opening in the heavens something was descending – a bird, a dove, flying down towards the Jordan to Jesus and John. As they watched, the dove rested on Jesus and then disappeared. Before they had time to think about these strange and wonderful sights, a voice thundered from above: 'This is my Son, whom I love; with him I am well pleased' (Matthew 3:17).

The Holy Spirit, who had just descended upon Jesus in bodily form, compelled him to walk into the wilderness. There was no choice – Jesus had surrendered his life to the calling of the Father. The choices had been settled. Now Jesus surrendered to being led, carried to every next step, until he faced the cross.

For now, the next step was the wilderness: fasting and making ready for his assault on the kingdom of darkness. He could stop eating, but he could not stop drinking. He stayed near water, not far from the wadis that led into the Jordan. These forty days were about settling his dependency upon his Father. He had surrendered his will to the will of his Father. Now he had to work out what that meant in practice. Did he meditate on the book of Deuteronomy – the three sermons Moses preached to prepare Jesus' namesake Joshua and the people of Israel to go into the Promised Land? I think so. What we know for sure is that when the devil came to call, Jesus used verses from Deuteronomy to silence his adversary and send him on his way.

'If you are the Son of God, tell this stone to become

bread' (Luke 4:3). Jesus knew he was the Son, and the Father had confirmed that fact to those who were listening at his baptism, but would he use his power to save himself? If he used his power to save himself now, hungry as he was, at the furthest point of human endurance – forty days without food – then he would always be open to the same temptation in the future. If he could not stand up under the test now, the suggestion that he should save himself from a cruel death on a cross in the future would surely have been too powerful.

Faced with the devil's trial, the words of Moses came to mind. Jesus, like the people of Israel waiting to enter the Promised Land, had been learning how God sustains the humble, even in the midst of a desert. 'Man does not live on bread alone but on every word that comes from the mouth of the LORD' (Deuteronomy 8:3).

Suddenly the scene changed. Where was he? On a mountain? In an instant, he could see the splendour of the nations. The devil knew he was master of all he surveyed and he would offer it to Jesus if he would only submit and bow down. Jesus knew that his call was to every nation – all people. He knew the kingdom that he had come to inaugurate was to challenge and change every other kingdom. The question was: could he wait on the Father's plan and process, or did he want it all now? Again, Deuteronomy came to mind. 'Fear the LORD your God, serve him only' (Deuteronomy 6:13).

Frustrated, but not finished, the devil took Jesus to the top of the Temple. 'Throw yourself off – you obviously know the Bible. You know that the Messiah will be protected, and that God will command angels to guard and keep you – like it says in Psalm 91.' Jesus saw the temptation for what it was, presented with its religious veneer. Would he make a show of his gifting and calling, or would he allow his Father to use him as he wanted, when he wanted? Deuteronomy again. 'Do not test the LORD your God' (Deuteronomy 6:16).

At the end of the temptations the angels fed him, the Spirit of God, on whom he would now depend, filled him with power and he walked out of the wilderness into the land, to conquer darkness and take the territory of human hearts as frontier posts of the kingdom.

Postscript

In the river, Jesus' identity had been settled; in the desert, his methods had been confirmed. He was ready.

The river and the desert were preparation for Jesus' ministry – preparation for his work of pioneering, planting, bridging and building. His baptism and temptation released the power and authority he needed to get the job done. It may be that the baptism was more to do with authority, the authority of surrender, and that the temptation was more to do with power, the power of submission. Jesus' preparation settled how he would use the power and exercise the authority. He would not use the power for himself, and he would not use the authority to aggrandize his position.

Reflections

If we are to model ourselves on the apostolic ministry of Jesus, we need to find ways of encountering and living within the presence of God as he did. Of course, as the Son of God he has a unique place and perspective, but as our master and guide he shows us the way. When we view the life of Jesus, we see that he is able to access the reality of his Father's presence and power in three different ways:

1. Through the trials, tests and temptations he faced on a daily basis.
2. Through the sudden outpouring of power as the kingdom quickly advanced.
3. Through the disciplines of prayer, solitude, silence and fasting.

If our lives are to flow with the same power and presence of God as we would recognize in the life of Christ, we must practise these three areas ourselves.

Within the landscape of our life, God's presence lies like an underground river or a seam of gold, running through the strata of our experience. To get at the water or gold, to reveal his underlying presence, the Lord will use three methods of exposure. These are:

1. Erosion – revealing God's presence through the erosive forces of life, i.e. the difficulties that we face.
2. Eruption – the sovereign outpouring of God's presence, often with explosive consequences.
3. Excavation – 'digging into' the life of God through the consistent application of 'the spiritual disciplines'.

1. Erosion

> Consider it pure joy, my brothers, whenever you face trials of
> many kinds, because you know that the testing of your faith
> develops perseverance. Perseverance must finish its work so
> that you may be mature and complete, not lacking anything.
> (James 1:2)

This passage (like others that use similar wording, e.g.
1 Peter 1:7; Romans 5:4) indicates the process by which
God's transforming presence changes us through difficulty and trial.

'The difference between temptation and trial is that
temptation will lead to us forgetting about God,
whereas trial will cause us to remember Him.' This is
something that Dietrich Bonhoeffer pointed out in his
little book *Temptations*. Bonhoeffer, one of the martyrs
of the twentieth century, was imprisoned and executed
by the Nazis in 1945. He knew about trials and how
they caused him to remember God (as his *Letters from
Prison* indicate). But he also knew about temptations
and how powerful they are in causing us to forget
about God. Anyone who has walked with God for any
length of time will be able to recognize the difference
between the two. God allows trials so that we remember him, and become more aware of his underlying
presence in our lives and more grateful for the prosperity his presence achieves.

Personal reflection

(a) Finding joy in trial is about focusing beyond the
    difficulty on the God who can use all things for our
    benefit and blessing. Do you do this?

(b) Sympathy may be helpful to those who struggle with life, but do we ever cause people to look beyond their experience to the maturity and completeness that it will produce?

(c) Those who do not know God will be surprised about our attitude towards trial and suffering, and the Bible tells us to be ready to explain this. Is our attitude to difficulty different from the world's, and do non-Christians have any reason to think that our faith works at times of trouble?

2. Eruption

The eruptive and explosive presence of God is a regular feature of the biblical story. God will, from time to time, pour out his presence upon his people. Such occasions are often accompanied by 'the mountain-top experience', e.g. Sinai, Zion, the Sermon on the Mount, the Mount of Transfiguration, Pentecost in Jerusalem. These events are expressions of God's decision, of his sovereign grace, rather than of our ability to work something up. God chooses from time to time and with differing degrees of intensity to meet his people.

Principally this experience is found in worship, where Jesus promises to manifest his presence and where the Bible testifies that God is pleased 'to inhabit' (see Matthew 18:20; Psalm 22:3). In recent years, encountering God in worship and expecting his overflowing presence has been the mainstay of the renewal movement, and it is one of the principal values of our life as a church.

Worship is intended by God to be a place where we

meet with him and where he is free to make his presence manifest. One of the most important effects of
meeting with God in worship is that such an experience
makes you hungry for his presence. In fact, one of the
tests of whether you have really met with God is
whether a desire emerges within you to return and
meet with him again.

Personal reflection

(a) Do you come expectantly to worship? Do you recognize that your expectancy will often define how
much of God's presence you experience?
(b) Are we checking our attitudes and our lives, confessing our sins so that God is pleased to be among
us, or do our lives present obstacles to the holiness
of God?
(c) Have we ever thought of inviting people to come
and meet with God rather than just come to church?

3. Excavation

Evangelical Christianity has in the past emphasized the
importance of a disciplined walk with God, but
because this became detached from an experience of
the manifest presence of God, discipline sometimes
became legalism, and this led to spiritual death.

In similar manner, evangelicals and Catholics alike
had a strong theology of testing and suffering producing growth in our spiritual lives, but again this was
sometimes without recognizing the life-giving experience of God's presence made real to us each day. This
became 'muscular Christianity' and meaningless effort.

Charismatic renewal has brought the eruption of God's presence back to the landscape of life, but we need to be sure that in correcting this imbalance we do not fall prey to the temptation of losing the other elements of the landscape.

We need a thorough understanding of erosion – the purpose of testing and trial in our life; eruption – the right expectations of faithful worship; and excavation – the grace-filled hard work of being a disciple of Jesus.

For 1,500 years the disciplines that produced the contemplative life were the mainstay of Christian spirituality. Silence, solitude, study, fasting, prayer and work were the backbone of Christian character and of growth towards godliness. Only in recent times have these begun to re-emerge as evangelicals and charismatics look back to the early centuries of the church to learn from their forebears how to live the Christian life.

Personal reflection

(a) Are we asking Jesus to make us disciples, i.e. 'disciplined ones', so that we become like him, or are we more like the crowd that followed Jesus – only around when times are easy?

(b) Are we looking to be discipled or only encouraged in our Christian life? Being discipled means becoming like someone who is further on in the process and becoming like Jesus. Is this our aim?

(c) If we want the presence of God in our daily lives, in our workplace and relationships, the only way we can be sure that this occurs is by committing ourselves to excavating his presence in the landscape of our life. He is always present – it is just that his presence is not always manifest.

(d) If the presence and power of Jesus were more obviously present with you, do you think that it would make any difference to your success and the lives of those around you?

3

Pioneer

Peter

The sun had been up for three hours and was warming the dusty streets of Jerusalem. Those living in the city had already put in almost half a day's work; those merely visiting on pilgrimage were milling around the streets as they waited for the events of the Feast of Weeks to unfold.

The sound came suddenly, and from everywhere – a roaring, like the sirocco winds rushing off the Arabian desert. The crowd stirred, some reaching for their head coverings to protect their faces from the anticipated dust storm, others looking around for shelter. The sound of the wind quickly subsided, to be replaced by another roar – people shouting at the tops of their voices, many voices all at once. Through the cacophony, words, even whole sentences, emerged, spoken in many different languages. The pilgrims from all around the world could hear declarations in their native tongues. The momentary confusion subsided into curiosity. What could this be? There on the flat roof of a house where the commotion was centred, a large man was stepping forward to speak to the crowd.

'Listen, we're not drunk. It's only nine o'clock in the morning. This is the fulfilment of the prophecy you've all been waiting for.' Peter held the crowd's attention as he reinterpreted the prophecies of the Old Testament, applying them to the recent events everyone had been talking about – the death of Jesus of Nazareth and the rumour of his resurrection. They continued to listen as Peter laid before them God's claim on their lives, challenging their collusion with the national authorities who had killed Jesus. They heard the troubling voice of God stirring their hearts. 'What shall we do?' they asked. Without breaking stride, and using the familiar words of Jesus, Peter said, 'Repent and be baptized.' Three thousand heeded the call and the church of Jesus Christ was born.

At the end of Luke's record of these momentous events (see Acts 2) he paints a picture of a remarkable church, a larger version of the community of the twelve disciples and Jesus. Jesus had planted the new community, Peter was pioneering its expansion. God had used Peter for this breakthrough. He was leading the rush to the new frontier, but there would be other breakthroughs that this frontiersman would also be used to make.

In Chapter 2 we saw that Jesus pioneered by:

• claiming lives as new territory for the kingdom of God;
• proclaiming the gospel to any who would hear;

- acting decisively with enemy counterattacks;
- operating in divine authority and power;
- establishing a bridgehead from which he could work.

All of these qualities and activities of apostolic ministry are important, and we could relate them to any of the New Testament apostles. To provide a context for a clearer understanding of pioneering work, however, I want to start in a somewhat unexpected place.

In 1776 Thomas Jefferson signed the Declaration of Independence. His signature, like that of his cosignatories, was intended to endorse and declare publicly the determination of the American people to seek freedom and self-determination. In 1803, as the president of the newly emerging United States, he signed another paper, but this time in secret – a message to Congress calling for an expedition to explore the westward land of the American continent. The message was secret because the land belonged to France. The expedition was necessary because a passage from east to west needed to be found. The aim was to navigate the Mississippi–Missouri rivers, find a way over the continental divide from their source and plot a passage to the Pacific Ocean.

Jefferson's plan was to send his personal secretary, Meriwether Lewis, and his close friend, William Clark, along with a dozen hand-picked men and a budget of 2,500 dollars. Yet even as the plans were being laid, Emperor Napoleon, in a surprise move, offered this whole western region (known as the Lousiana Territory) to Jefferson for the price of 15 million dollars.

The USA suddenly grew by one million square miles! Now all of the land to be explored by the Lewis–Clark expedition, from the Mississippi to the Rockies and from the Rockies to the western seaboard, was part of the United States.

Lewis kept a diary of his team's exploits – recording their difficulties and privations, discoveries and break-throughs – which, when published in the settlements of the eastern seaboard, fuelled the fire for the westward expansion of America. There are few people who have ever followed in their footsteps, but their pioneering exploits led to one of the great achievements of human history – the settling of the American West.

Like all pioneers, Lewis claimed new territory, spread the good news, acted decisively, provided a way for others to follow in his footsteps, and operated within his delegated authority. These all reflect the traits of pioneering ministry in the life of Jesus and represent well the work of people like Peter and Paul. Each of these elements would probably pass without much comment, except the issue of authority. This is undoubtedly the area that creates the most contention.

All pioneers (whether they be the apostle Peter or Meriwether Lewis) require power and authority to explore and establish new frontiers: power – the provision and release of all that is needed for the venture; and authority – the delegated freedom and opportunity to exercise the power that has been given.

Lewis's power and authority were given to him largely through his relationship with the president of the United States. Peter's was given to him through his relationship with Jesus, who authorized, resourced and equipped his mission. Of course, the ability to exercise authority and wield power (whether human or divine) effectively will depend on a person's maturity. The more complete the person, the more effective the pioneer. Lewis was a man who had matured through the experiences of life. Peter matured in similar fashion, although the most important period of this maturation took place during his time among the Twelve. Of these three years, during which he was personally discipled by Jesus, the most important period was his time of failure and personal brokenness. In the kingdom, a recognition of personal weakness is a prerequisite for the exercise of power and authority.

We can learn much from the pioneers of human history, but if we are to be pioneers for the kingdom of God, or part of a pioneering movement led by others, we would do well to learn from the likes of Peter. Authority and power released from the hand of God are more important than education or status. Maturity and character worked into the life of a believer are more important than charm or personal ability.

One day, Peter and John were on their way to the Temple. Their plan was to pray. As they went through the Court of the Gentiles to the Beautiful Gate, they passed by the groups of beggars with their various petitions. It was the same scene as usual, met by any worshipper on any day. One man, ankles and legs bent and crippled from birth, was being carried by his helpers to his usual place. He called out to Peter and John. Perhaps because he was still being carried, they noticed him among the crowd and heard him over the din. Something in Peter stirred. He had watched Jesus on numerous occasions do the same – 'seeing what the Father was doing'. Now it was his turn. What was this indefinable feeling emerging in his heart – faith? He looked at the man and said, 'Look at me! I don't have any money, but I do have this: Get up!' As he reached out and took him by the hand, the man's ankles and feet immediately strengthened. His legs straightened and he leaped to a standing position, something he had never done in his forty years of life (see Acts 3).

The pioneer was at it again, crashing through the boundaries. This was the Temple, the most holy place. A crowd had gathered, drawn by the now healed beggar, leaping and screaming like a banshee, and so Peter began to preach. In the middle of his sermon, in which he was trying to explain his role in the healing and God's purposes within it, Peter was arrested (see Acts 4). As so often with a pioneering push for a new frontier, the enemy's reaction was swift: the Temple soldiers, pushing past the avid listeners, took Peter and John away to prison, to be questioned by the Sanhedrin. The rulers and elders saw the soaring faith and powerful anointing on Peter and John, and interpreted it as human courage, but still they were impressed and took note that these ordinary, uneducated men were disciples of Jesus. This was yet another breakthrough – into the ruling classes and the priestly caste. The result of all this was that there would be more people confessing Christ as Lord, a rapidly growing church, and priests now being numbered among the disciples (see Acts 6:7).

Interestingly, these two breakthroughs of Peter's – among the ordinary people and the religious leaders –

mirror the bridgeheads established by Jesus in his ministry as he opened frontier posts for the kingdom in Galilee and Jerusalem, one among the populace as he declared the kingdom and healed the sick, the other among the elite as he proclaimed God's righteousness and drove the traders from the Temple. The first established an opportunity for him to work among the mixed crowds that were found in Galilee. The second opened the way for him to take his message to the centre and seat of power – the Jerusalem hierarchy. Peter was a pioneer along with the other twelve apostles, but the initial breach had already been made by another: the apostle and high priest of our calling, Jesus.

Peter was an apostle, and as such he was someone who had been given a special gift of divine power to break through barriers and open long-established strongholds. The power was obviously God's power, but it came in both word and deed. It seemed to offer Peter both a command of particular situations and protection while in the midst of them. In the same way, it appears that apostolic pioneers today continue to operate with an unusual level of power and protection. Protection is related to power as power is related to authority. Perhaps the best way to think of protection is as a feature of power, or even an expression of it. It is important, however, to recognize that power and protection are not constant features of an apostle's life. Even in the ministry of Jesus there appears to have been an ebb and flow (see Luke 5:17). Jesus was reliant on what his Father was doing – he only did what he saw the Father doing (see John 5:19) – and so the Father gave him power through the presence of the Holy Spirit, as the need arose. The pioneer depends on his relationship with Jesus for the impartation of power, which will flow as the Lord chooses to release it.

Authority and submission

Power is vital. For an apostle to function effectively, this is the principal requirement, but for power to be wielded effectively, a person also needs authority. In the Scriptures, power and authority are always paired together. Power is the resource to act; authority is the right to use the power that has been given. We have seen that the key to authority is surrender; the key to power is submission. These are usually worked into the life of a person through testing and trial, developing a life that is humbly available to the will of God. These are the vital prerequisites for anyone seeking to develop an apostolic calling, and can be seen in the life of Jesus, Peter and any other biblical pioneer or apostle.

To understand this more completely, we will need to look at other apostolic figures and seek to come to an understanding of how authority and power work in an apostolic calling.

Paul

He was on a mission from God. He knew what he had to do – find the heretics and bring them before the authorities for trial. He had been given special letters of dispensation to hunt them down wherever they were hidden, and he was on his way to Damascus to do precisely that.

Suddenly a light flashed around him and he was thrown to the ground. Had his horse shied as lightning struck? He could not tell – all he knew was that he was unable to see. As he groped on the ground, a voice addressed him: 'Saul, Saul, why do you persecute me?' Who was that? Was it one of the heretics? Then came the answer: 'I am Jesus, whom you are persecuting' (Acts 9:4–5). In a moment of revelation Saul realized that when he hurt the followers of Jesus, Jesus somehow experienced the pain; when he harmed his followers, Jesus felt it. He realized that Jesus and his followers were inextricably connected.

In Damascus, blind and desperate for God to do something, the new convert waited. Three days later, Ananias – a brave and obedient follower – came to baptize Saul and pray for him to be filled with the Holy Spirit. The message he brought from the Lord was about how much he would have to suffer to fulfil his mission to the Gentiles. Almost immediately, the trials began. Understandably, the infant church was suspicious of this new convert, who had once pursued them to death. Unsurprisingly, the religious authorities now made him public enemy number one. Paul had to learn to manage pretty much by himself, and yet apparently his new passion was undiminished.

Five times I received from the Jews the forty lashes minus one. Three times I was beaten with rods, once I was stoned, three times I was shipwrecked, I spent a night and a day in the open sea, I have been constantly on the move. I have been in danger from rivers, in danger from bandits, in danger from my own countrymen, in danger from Gentiles; in danger in the city, in danger in the country, in danger at sea; and in danger from false brothers. I have laboured and toiled and have often gone without sleep; I have known hunger and thirst and have often gone without food; I have been cold and naked. (2 Corinthians 11:24–7)

When we compare this list of trials with the story of Paul's exploits in the Acts of the Apostles (e.g. Acts 14:5; 14:19–20; 16:22–4; 19:30–31), we discover that most of the terrible things described in 2 Corinthians occurred before his public ministry really got under way. It would appear that most of the events spoken of in 2 Corinthians took place during the so-called 'hidden years' of Paul, when for something between nine and thirteen years he drops out of the narrative of the Acts of the Apostles. He was obviously active during this time, and from the list of his sufferings clearly saw great opposition. He may well have been excommunicated from synagogues several times for preaching the gospel. Excommunication was usually marked by 39 lashes. Even if we consider 2 Corinthians to have been written by Paul in Rome (see Acts 28:16), most of the events still took place before his story is told in Acts.

Forty lashes minus one (five times), beaten with rods (three times), shipwrecked (three times) – at least these took place before Barnabas found Paul in Tarsus and took him to Antioch to help with the burgeoning work of the first Gentile church. Histories of the apostles' lives written in the second and third centuries speak of Paul's condition when Barnabas found him living in a cave in the mountains above Tarsus – half blind, bow-legged and bent over, all as a result of the many cruel beatings he had received. The young, vital man who had fallen from his horse on the way to Damascus had become old before his time, but this physically weakened, frail and broken man became an instrument of incredible power in the hands of God. The life that was all but snuffed out became the torch that lit the fires of a new life that burn among the Gentile peoples to this day.

After his period of apostolic training in the encouraging hands of Barnabas, Paul was sent with his mentor and friend on the first recorded apostolic mission to the Gentile world. The Holy Spirit said, 'Set apart for me Barnabas and Saul . . .' (Acts 13:2), and so they were sent. Paul, whose Jewish friends still knew him as Saul, now took his more recognizable name of Paul and began his life's work. It progressed with an incredible level of authority and power, and a horrendous level of trial and pain. Rejected, persecuted, even left for dead, Paul knew the daily strain of pushing back the frontiers of the kingdom and yet, in the midst of it all, he knew the gracious strengthening presence of Jesus and the protection and power he needed to get the job done. No wonder he was able to pen the words found in 1 Corinthians 2:1–5:

> When I came to you, brothers, I did not come with eloquence or superior wisdom as I proclaimed to you the testimony about God. For I resolved to know nothing while I was with you except Jesus Christ and him crucified. I came to you in weakness and fear, and with much trembling. My message and my preaching were not with wise and persua-

sive words, but with a demonstration of the Spirit's power, so that your faith might not rest on men's wisdom, but on God's power.

Proclamation of the gospel is obviously important, but without the 'demonstration of the Spirit's power' the breakthrough is not achieved. Interestingly, however, power is not found without weakness. Authority is not exercised without submission. Although Paul, like us, wished it were another way, this appears to be the pattern of apostolic ministry. Paul tells us:

> Three times I pleaded with the Lord to take it away from me. But he said to me, 'My grace is sufficient for you, for my power is made perfect in weakness.' Therefore I will boast all the more gladly about my weaknesses, so that Christ's power may rest on me. (2 Corinthians 12:8–9)

To summarize, it would appear that apostolic ministry:

- is a call to pioneer a new frontier;
- comes with the provision of authority and power;
- comes with divine protection;
- requires submission;
- flows from weakness.

Can we say that these statements are always true? Most people would recognize the pioneering nature of apostolic ministry and the presence of divine power and authority in their lives. But what about the other statements, those that deal with protection, submission and weakness? I think so. The witness of Scripture, the testimony of history and contemporary examples seem to lead to the same conclusions.

Historical and contemporary examples

When we think of divine protection for apostolic work, several contemporary examples come to mind. Brother Andrew was specially called and equipped to take the gospel to communist countries. On countless occasions, while smuggling Bibles across the border into Eastern bloc countries, he was given remarkable protection as border guards were blinded to the obvious presence of Bibles in his VW Beetle. Jackie Pullinger, living and working among the drug dens of the Walled City of Hong Kong, was given remarkable provisions of power to see captive lives transformed, and protection as she ministered as a single woman in some of the most violent streets of the world.

When we consider the subject of weakness expressed through human frailty, there are many clear examples. Take John Wesley – a man of extraordinary anointing, recognized by many as 'an apostle to the nation'. He struggled constantly with human frailty, trials and difficulties, both within his home and outside it. On one occasion, one of Wesley's friends walked into his lounge to discover Wesley's wife pulling him round the room by his hair, the same woman who later wrote an article attacking her husband in the London *Times*.

John Wimber, a great example to many of us, suffered taunts and attacks inside and outside the church. Some of his detractors seem to have devoted large portions of their lives to undermining him. Also he seemed to struggle daily with his health, and yet his apostolic ministry spawned a movement, started a denomination and touched the world.

My own experience, though far less significant than any mentioned above, has only been released through difficulty and trials, which have produced a continuing sense of human frailty and submission to God. As a young minister, I desperately wanted God to make a breakthrough among the young people with whom I worked. A silent, continuous and desperate prayer of 'God, please do something' framed my every action. The answer to this prayer came through some surprising circumstances.

While I was cutting the grass in my back garden to clear an area where our first child could play, I came across some ants' nests inhabited by the biting variety. Notwithstanding my respect for creation, I felt they would have to die. The only problem was that I could not think how to kill them. Finally I settled on the idea of petrol. Having poured it liberally over the nests (which I am sure would have been enough in itself to kill them), I began a search for matches.

I do not know whether it was the Lord trying to stop me from my headlong pursuit of disaster, but it took me an awfully long time to find some. When in the end I found the matches and struck one near the ants' nests, I hardly needed to throw it to find myself surrounded by an encircling conflagration. The petrol can was already alight when I decided to move it. For some reason I dropped it and the spout, alight and functioning like a flamethrower, gushed flaming petrol over my legs. Realizing that the only course of action was to undress as quickly as possible, I flicked off my shoes and began to remove my trousers, at the same time calling out to God for help.

By some amazing and miraculous happenstance, the flames went out and I assumed that I was free from danger. In fact, although the damage was not extensive, I had inflicted third-degree burns on myself and had to spend several weeks in an isolation room waiting for skin grafts. This was undoubtedly the lowest point of my life, but as I lay in the bed, cut off from all normal interaction with others, trying to read or listen to tapes, God began to unravel my perception of ministry. Unless he was doing the work through me, little or nothing of value would be achieved, and none of the breakthroughs that I was seeking would be seen.

I left the hospital a changed man. Within a few weeks, much to my surprise, I saw an incredible release of authority in preaching and power in ministry. My first experience of this was taking a youth weekend for a friend, who on his own admission was struggling with his church youth group. Something happened that I had never seen before, as people listened to my often faltering attempts to communicate. They came under the conviction of the Spirit, some weeping, others rooted to the spot. Of the twenty-six or so young people present, something like twenty-four came into a living experience of faith that weekend, and six or so have gone on to full-time ministry. This was not my usual experience up to that point, but since then God has done many similar things. I have discovered that God is able to achieve more in one anointed day than in twenty years of human endeavour.

The recognition of the importance of weakness and submission is fundamental to the biblical pattern of apostolic ministry, but does this mean that we should constantly expect trials and difficulties that bring an experience of breaking to our lives? My answer would be that, once broken, a person does not need to revisit the experience at such an intense level. There will be many reminders as we choose to follow Christ, but hopefully not too many cataclysms.

Watchman Nee, the great Chinese teacher and church leader, had a good illustration. One of his students was asking him about weakness and the experience of brokenness. He wanted to know whether he would have to repeat his painful experiences constantly to maintain a submissive position before the Lord. Nee took a biscuit from the table, broke it in two and carefully rejoined the pieces on the palm of one hand. He invited the student to reach out and touch the biscuit. Immediately the break was revealed, with the lightest of touches. He encouraged his student by saying that once broken, God need only touch the life of his servants to bring them back to a knowledge of their weakness.

Reflections

Therefore, since we are surrounded by such a great crowd of witnesses, let us throw off everything that hinders and the sin that so easily entangles, and let us run with perseverance the race marked out for us. Let us fix our eyes on Jesus, the author and perfecter of our faith . . . (Hebrews 12:1–2)

As 'author and perfecter', Jesus is both initiator and completer, pioneer and settler. He is the model for both, so obviously both are just as important as each other. The question is, which one are you – pioneer or settler? Below you will find some information and questions that should help you decide which one you are. Hopefully this will affirm you in your personal calling and equip you to function more effectively in the corporate calling of the church.

- A pioneer is someone who enjoys change and finds the stress of doing new things exciting rather than threatening. Pioneers are those who naturally reach out beyond their current experiences and relationships to discover new frontiers and challenges, and who find themselves frustrated by the disciplines needed to sustain what has already been established.
- Settlers have a great desire to grow what has been planted and develop what has been begun. There is a commitment to conserve, strengthen and 'flesh out' what has been initiated.

God uses the pioneers to initiate new work and the settlers to establish it. Most people would recognize the value of both initiating and establishing work within the kingdom, but God tends to use us most regularly in either one way or the other. We tend to gravitate towards one end of the pioneer–settler continuum. This is to be expected and affirmed.

- Do you enjoy change?
- Are you adaptable to new environments?

- Do you find yourself becoming bored when you spend 'too long' doing the same thing?
- Do you respond quickly to fresh insights?
- Do you enjoy the challenge of a new situation?
- Are you able to make quick decisions?

If you answered 'yes' to most of these questions, you are probably a pioneer.

- Do you appreciate careful preparation?
- Do you like to bring others along in any new work you start?
- Do you like to have an idea of the outcome before you start a new project?
- Do you work through the details before you act?
- Do you always try to finish what you have begun?
- Are you committed to hold on to what you have already established?

If you answered 'yes' to these questions, you are probably a settler.

You may, of course, find it difficult to answer these questions definitively. This could be for a number of reasons, but the most common one that I have encountered is that a pioneer is going through a settling phase, or a settler is going through a pioneering phase.

Undoubtedly, being forced out of our familiar zone of operation puts us under pressure, but when this happens we grow the most. I have found that when God causes a pioneer to settle, they mature more than they would if left alone – and vice versa. Therefore, if God is calling you to an apostolic ministry (which will almost certainly involve a pioneering element), do not be surprised if he forces you to settle for a time, to learn the strengths of this vital part of his overall ministry. You will learn how to value the role of the settlers, how to integrate their strengths into an apostolic work and, perhaps most importantly, how to ensure that what has been begun actually lasts.

4

Planter

Paul

The journey through Asia Minor had been different from what he had expected. Paul had new companions. The gap left with the departure of Barnabas, his old friend and partner in mission, had been filled first by Silas and then by Timothy. Different people meant different conversations. New people to relate to meant new things to think about.

The journey had been different for other reasons as well. The Lord had specifically intervened, and had prevented Paul from entering the province of Asia, which had Ephesus at its heart. God had then further cut down Paul's options by revealing that Bithynia was also not one of his chosen destinations. The only way open seemed to lead to the sea. In time, therefore, Paul and his companions came to Troas – the principal port of the northwest region.

What did God have in mind as the next step? Was this to be the site of a new congregation? Were they to head south on the coastal road to the population centres of Smyrna and Ephesus? Should they strike inland for the provincial capital of Pergamum? Should they catch a boat?

While they were in Troas, it appears that they met Luke.[1] We are not sure why Luke was in Troas, but it may have been due in part to the fact that the main centre of medical science in the world at that time was just up the road at Pergamum. Anyone visiting Pergamum would almost certainly have had to travel through Troas. Luke, the Christian doctor, would be a great asset to Paul and his friends. They could hardly have known the significance of Luke's friendship at that time, but no doubt they recognized in him an excellent new team member.

No doubt Paul had been asking important questions. Where was he to go next? What was God's plan for him and his new team? It seemed that so far the Lord had only said what he could not do and where he could not go. Nonetheless, Paul had learnt to be content in all circumstances (see Philippians 4:11–12) and over the years this had no doubt helped him to sleep when the opportunity arose, and to rest in the knowledge of God's sovereignty. So it was perhaps a surprise to find that God chose Paul's dreams to be the place of revelation. In the night, a man dressed as a Macedonian came to Paul in a vision, pleading with him, 'Come over to Macedonia and help us' (Acts 16:9). At last the waiting

---

[1] As the writer of the Acts of the Apostles, Luke gently inserts the first of the 'we' passages (see Acts 16:10) indicating that he, the writer, was now a participant in the adventure.

was over. Paul now had the fresh direction he had been anticipating.

Travelling to Macedonia from Troas was not a problem. Ships left every day to sail along this principal sea route, so it was simply a matter of finding a boat leaving at the time they required. The historical name for Troas was Alexandria, after the great empire builder Alexander the Great. They would leave the city of his name and sail to the place of his birth – Macedonia, the historical fountainhead of Graeco-Roman culture and the first republic of the Empire. Whether Paul and his companions knew it or not, this was one of the most strategically important moments in the history of Christian mission. The first recorded attempt to extend the frontiers of the kingdom into Europe had begun.

Sailing from Troas, skirting the island of Samothrace, Paul's ship put in at Neapolis and then he and his companions continued their journey to the capital, Philippi. There Paul found a wealthy and cosmopolitan city, one that had flourished as the Roman Empire had grown. In the past gold mining had established its prosperity and the association with Alexander the Great had secured its importance. Now its status was determined by the fact that it was a wealthy retirement community. Philippi was set in lush farmland, portions of which were given to Roman soldiers as part of their retirement package on leaving the imperial army.

Even though he had spent some time in Troas, becoming familiar with the distinctive feel of an established Roman colony, still Philippi must have been an alien and challenging prospect for Paul, the Jew from Tarsus. Unlike the ancient cities and towns of the eastern Mediterranean, known for their colour, chaos and vibrancy, Philippi was a strangely ordered place, like a modern planned community. Roman law was absolute there, and the populace were committed to maintaining their wealth and enjoying its fruits. Although most people were conversant in the common tongue, Greek, hardly anyone spoke it. This was a Roman city and proud of it, so people spoke in the elegant and cultured tongue of their Latin forebears.

Paul had developed a methodology for reaching cities. He would begin with the synagogue, sharing a scriptural insight as the visiting rabbi who had the status and credibility of having been personally trained by the great Gamaliel. As often as he had opportunity, he would speak of the fulfilment of messianic expectation in the person of Jesus. Here in this new place of God's calling, however, there were so few Jews that a synagogue could not legally be established. (The rabbinical rules said that there needed to be ten Jewish men for synagogue worship.) This city was a different kettle of fish from anywhere else that Paul had tried to reach. He was entering an environment where people were difficult to converse with, ignorant of the Scriptures and completely indifferent to his message. Yet he was certain that the Lord wanted him to plant a church there in Macedonia. He would have to return to the first principles of mission and evangelism that Jesus had taught to his disciples to achieve success in this new mission.

Mission strategy of Jesus

Jesus had a clear strategy of mission and evangelism, which is recorded for us in the first three Gospels. It has four parts – time, team, target and task.

Time

Timing was tremendously important to Jesus, as we saw in Chapter 2. A principal part of his proclamation of the kingdom was to do with God's time. Throughout his life, he modelled to the disciples the need to operate within God's timing, to the extent that he would remove himself from places of opposition because 'the time was not right' for him to be arrested and killed. He would choose the right time to address individuals like Levi and Zacchaeus, so that the kingdom could come to them. Similarly, he revealed to the disciples that there was a timing for them within the mission in which God had called them to participate. When he sent out the Twelve, it appears to have taken place at a moment of great fruitfulness in his ministry – a time to multiply the mission. When he sent out the Seventy-two, it appears to have come at a time when Jesus was already making plans for his final journey to Jerusalem, when the task was more about completing the mission. The timing was significant in both cases.

Paul, like any other apostolic individual, understood that timing was fundamental to the success of his mission. He needed a combination of practical wisdom, to recognize the opportunities as they arose, and revelation of God's 'now moment', to be able to operate confidently in God's time.

Team

To fulfil the task successfully, Jesus formed his disciples into the simplest of teams – he sent them out in pairs. Human beings are social creatures, designed by God to work together for a common end. The Bible has many references relating to the importance of partnership. One book that has several helpful insights is Ecclesiastes. What it says undergirds Jesus' practice.

- When two or more people apply themselves to a common task, a *synergy* is produced – an 'extra something'.

  Two are better than one, because they have a good return for their work. (Ecclesiastes 4:9)

- There is a *safety* in numbers which ensures that disasters are never met alone and help is always on hand.

  If one falls down, his friend can help him up. But pity the man who falls and has no-one to help him up! (Ecclesiastes 4:10)

- There is a *security* to be found when more than one person engages in a joint project.

  If two lie down together, they will keep warm. But how can one keep warm alone? (Ecclesiastes 4:11)

- There is a *strength* to be found in the company of others.

Though one may be overpowered, two can defend themselves. (Ecclesiastes 4:12)

- As well as all this, because we are designed for inter-
  dependence rather than independence, for inte-
  grated rather than isolated lives, God appears to add
  his presence to a company of believers or community of faith, however small, so that there is a *spiritual reality* which is revealed also.

A cord of three strands is not quickly broken. (Ecclesiastes 4:12)

This last point is underlined by Jesus when he says that
he is present in the midst of disciples who choose to live
and work together, and that requests made by these
believers will be heard in heaven.

Again, I tell you that if two of you on earth agree about anything you ask for, it will be done for you by my Father in
heaven. For where two or three come together in my name,
there am I with them. (Matthew 18:19–20)

Following the example of Jesus, Paul rarely worked
alone. The 'one-man band' is very much the exception
and not the rule. There were a few occasions when
circumstances necessitated a solitary approach, but given
the option, Paul, like all the other apostles and evangelists of the New Testament, chose to work with others.

Target

In modelling mission strategy to his disciples (both the
Twelve and the Seventy-two), Jesus gave clear targets

to his teams. These began with the general and moved to the specific. First, a place (i.e. a geographical location) and/or a specific people group was identified.

> The Lord . . . sent them two by two ahead of him to every town and place where he was about to go. (Luke 10:1)

> Do not go among the Gentiles or enter any town of the Samaritans. Go rather to the lost sheep of Israel. (Matthew 10:5–6)

Then an individual person was targeted.

> When you enter a house, first say, 'Peace to this house.' If a man of peace is there, your peace will rest on him; if not, it will return to you. Stay in that house, eating and drinking whatever they give you, for the worker deserves his wages. Do not move around from house to house. (Luke 10:5–7)

> Whatever town or village you enter, search for some worthy person there and stay at his house until you leave. (Matthew 10:11)

In this way, Jesus revealed God's unseen hand in the mission field. He was ahead of them, preparing key relationships with particular individuals in specific areas so that the work of extending the frontiers of the kingdom could be completed.

Paul usually found his key person in the synagogue in which he preached in any given town. Philippi would be different. He could be sure, however, that this key relationship would somehow be there, because he was certain that God had sent him.

Task

In defining the task, Jesus gave his disciples a job description which arose from his own ministry. He authorized, empowered and commissioned them to say what he had said and to do what he had done. He did not restrict their work to words alone, but called them to exercise both the words and the works of the kingdom.

> Heal the sick who are there and tell them, 'The kingdom of God is near you.' (Luke 10:9)

> As you go, preach this message: 'The kingdom of heaven is near.' Heal the sick, raise the dead, cleanse those who have leprosy, drive out demons. Freely you have received, freely give. (Matthew 10:7-8)

Paul was familiar with the proclamation and demonstration of the gospel and knew that breaking through new frontiers would require kingdom power. This appears to have been a settled issue for him and part of his daily expectation. Nonetheless, the question remained: how and where would it all start?

Breakthrough in Philippi

Undoubtedly, Paul knew the model of mission taught by Jesus, and knew that the principles he had learnt were applicable in every circumstance. Whether the environment included the presence of a synagogue or not, he would be able to adapt and operate effectively. Equipped with this understanding, Paul and his team began the task of planting their first church on European soil.

Paul had spent a few days in Philippi, no doubt making a thorough investigation of the city, looking for the opportunities and options available. At first sight, it had not appeared especially fertile ground. Yet Paul knew that if there was anyone in the city who had any knowledge of the Scriptures (and who would therefore provide an opportunity for witness and a starting point for planting), he would find them gathered near a flowing river, outside the city walls. This was standard practice for both devout Jews and 'God-fearers' (those Gentiles who had come to honour the Scriptures and believe in the God of Israel). The flowing river would provide ample water for the ceremonial washing which was symbolic of the spiritual process of cleansing from sin and was needed within the worship of Jews at the time. So Paul had looked for such a place. 'On the Sabbath we went outside the city gate to the river, where we expected to find a place of prayer' (Acts 16:13a).

Paul expected to find the place of prayer, partly because he expected some breakthrough, certain as he was of God's specific calling to Philippi, but also because he used his own practical experience and wisdom. When he found the place, the next step was to adopt the role of the rabbi, taking the familiar seated position to teach and speaking to those who would listen. 'We sat down and began to speak to the women who had gathered there' (Acts 16:13b).

It must have been great for the other members of Paul's team to watch him apply the mission principles of Jesus in such a new and challenging environment. As he taught, he would watch his audience closely, looking for evidence of responsiveness. Who was the prepared person of peace? It was obviously not a man, because only women were present. 'One of those listening was a woman named Lydia, a dealer in purple cloth from the city of Thyatira, who was a worshipper of God' (Acts 16:14a).

Philippi was a place that attracted traders and merchants from all around the world. This wealthy Roman community could afford the best. Lydia sold the purple cloth of Asia Minor, prized throughout the world as the finest and most desirable clothing fabric. Such a trade would have made her a person of considerable status within the community. It was this person whom the Lord was touching. 'The Lord opened her heart to respond to Paul's message' (Acts 16:14b).

What next? Jesus had said, 'Stay with the man of peace – the worthy person.' But surely the Lord could not expect his team of men to stay with a woman? Would it not leave them open to the suggestion of immorality and scandal? Interestingly, without any prompting, Lydia behaved as Jesus predicted a person of peace would. 'When she and the members of her household were baptised, she invited us to her home' (Acts 16:15a).

No doubt Paul was reluctant. However high her status, she was still a new believer – and a woman – and tongues would almost certainly wag. Yet he knew the directive of the Lord. 'Stay in that house, eating and drinking whatever they give you' (Luke 10:7). So he relented. '"If you consider me a believer in the Lord,"

she said, "come and stay at my house." And she per-
suaded us' (Acts 16:15b).

The mission strategy of Jesus had proved successful
yet again. His intention that new believers should
be sought and found and gathered into a believing
community was again fulfilled. As a church-planting
strategy, Paul's experience in Philippi bears little
resemblance to what you might read in current litera-
ture, and yet it was undoubtedly successful and firmly
based on the pattern that Jesus had given.

In Chapter 2 we identified Jesus as the original
apostle and summarized his work as a planter in the
following way. He:

- recognized the right time to plant;
- identified the people who could open doors to other
  relationships;
- prioritized relationship over popularity;
- focused his energy and gifts into a small, gathered
  group;
- imparted a pattern of community life that could
  grow and multiply all by itself.

Paul the planter recognized the right time to act through
the vision of the Macedonian man. He identified the one
who would open doors to other relationships in the
person of Lydia. He prioritized his relationship with her
and the new believers, even though others might have
misunderstood his intentions.

Like all successful church-planters, Paul was
extremely focused. He knew that the key was to pour his
life into the new community being established by God.

He knew that as he poured his life into their life, what God had put into him would be transferred to them. And so, after the conversion of Lydia and her household, we find Paul making regular trips to the place of prayer. Had the church already outgrown Lydia's home? Had the intention always been for a public meeting in the open air that could be followed up in households? We are uncertain of the details and reasons, but the account is clear. Paul returned to the original meeting place again and again (see Acts 16:16–18).

Such was his focus that when he was troubled by a slave girl who was captive to a powerful demon of prediction and fortune-telling, he attempted to ignore her, even though she was screaming at the top of her voice. It became a daily occurrence: Paul and his companions would gather with the new believers and their contacts (probably during the siesta hours under the shade of trees by the river) and the demon which the young girl carried would call out, stirred by the presence of God. In nurturing and developing this church plant, there was no benefit to be found in casting out that demon, and so Paul sought to ignore it. Eventually, however, the situation became impossible and Paul, operating with divine authority and power, cast out the demon, freed the girl – and brought trouble down on his own head.

My own assessment is that Paul sensed that there was no grace within the situation to further the kingdom or promote the gospel. He recognized that there was no openness in the slave girl's owners, so he chose to stick with the open door that God had provided rather than try to force open others. In that sense he demonstrated the focus, commitment and discipline necessary to be a successful church-planter. As it turned out, God had a hidden plan to reveal his other person of peace through these circumstances.

Paul and Silas were dragged before the Roman magistrates by the slave girl's owners. With her demonic insight, she was a much prized commodity: she seems to have been owned by a cartel who, in that indolent and leisured retirement community, earned a great deal of money from her so-called 'gifts'. No doubt looking for retribution, these local businessmen demanded summary Roman justice. Paul and Silas were beaten and thrown into the city jail. God's plan was still unfolding: he intended to add another household to the Philippian church before Paul and Silas moved on in their missionary journey. During the night, choosing to ignore the pain from their beating and their dire circumstances, Paul and Silas sang praises to God. What happened next was remarkable by any estimate.

I can remember hearing Jack Hayford speak of an African-American preacher who seemed to describe the situation well: 'Their songs rose from the cell, penetrated the prison walls, were carried to heaven's courts and into the throne room of the Lord himself, who on hearing their song began to tap his feet, and there was an earthquake in Philippi!'

The jailer, thinking that all the prisoners had escaped through the now open doors, was about to kill himself by falling on his own sword. Paul stopped him, convincing him that no one had left and that suicide was unnecessary. The jailer was immediately brought under the conviction of the Spirit and asked them how he might be saved. On this occasion it was not very hard to spot the person of peace and so Paul led him to the Lord along with his whole household, baptizing them all immediately. Paul and Silas would soon leave Philippi, but now there was a substantial church with at least two key households at its heart. Although his own presence within Philippi had become untenable, Paul was able to leave Luke and Timothy to continue with the process of discipleship and the imparting of a pattern of community life.

The astonishing thing for contemporary church-planters working in the West is that Paul was able to achieve so much in such a short time. This can be explained by the level of apostolic anointing that undoubtedly rested on Paul, and by the fact that he stayed so close to the method taught and modelled by Jesus. Paul knew how to recognize the time, how to use a team, how to identify the target and how to implement the task. Yet the anointing, the methods and the practical wisdom available to Paul were all gifts of God.

Some years later, Paul penned these words: 'For we are God's workmanship, created in Christ Jesus to do good works, which God prepared in advance for us to do' (Ephesians 2:10). This verse comes within one of the most comprehensive expositions of grace in the New Testament. Paul unequivocally teaches that salvation is by grace: it is a gift of God. He underlines this truth by stating clearly that human effort has no part to play. 'For it is by grace you have been saved, through faith – and this not from yourselves, it is the gift of God – not by works, so that no-one can boast' (Ephesians 2:8–9).

Having made this absolutely clear, Paul goes on to explain the nature of the relationship between God's grace and our call. We have been created for a task; we have a design and a calling. 'For we are God's workmanship . . .' But all of this has been 'given' – in other words, it comes 'by grace'. To fulfil our destiny, we have to live out who we are designed to be. We act on what God has done, but even these actions have been prepared 'in advance' – these too have been given by God and are manifestations of his grace.

What Paul taught, he lived. The church in Philippi was a work of God from beginning to end. By grace, God revealed to Paul his timing. By grace, he developed Paul's sense of anticipation through general guidance and particular revelation. By grace, God gave Paul the right team for a successful mission. By grace, the target became clear as God revealed the key relationships within Philippi. By grace, God opened the hearts of individuals so that Paul had the opportunity to fulfil his task of proclaiming the gospel.

By the time Paul arrived in Philippi, he had learnt how to apply the grace of God to the daily outworkings of his calling. The resources of grace supplied in different ways were working together to produce a fruitful harvest. The process that culminated in the church being planted in Philippi began with Jesus directing Paul on the road through Asia Minor. 'Having been kept by the Holy Spirit from preaching the word in the province of Asia . . . they tried to enter Bithynia, but the Spirit of Jesus would not allow them to' (Acts 16:6–7).

Many believe that this was Paul's only *modus operandi*, and that in each situation he simply waited for information that the Spirit of God would give him. In fact, Paul had two elements to his decision-making process. One was the daily revelation of the Holy Spirit, and the other was the principles and patterns of mission and ministry that he carried with him from place to place. As these two indispensable components of divine guidance worked in his life, he was able to apply the grace of God to each new context and watch for how God was continuing to work in each new situation. For example, Paul clearly had the mission strategy of Jesus available to him when he arrived in Philippi. What he did not know was who the person of peace was meant to be. For this he required the insight given by the Holy Spirit, who was working through him to see a church planted in Philippi.

The evidence of Paul's life teaches us that we need to know how to access grace within each fresh challenge. We can do this by learning this framework of mission applicable to every new circumstance, and relying on the Holy Spirit for daily resources and revelation. When we become settled about these things, our work becomes less complicated. We know that we do not have to ask God for fresh principles, only insights on how to apply them. We know that we do not have to ask God for a new pattern, only people, places and a manifestation of his power.

Reflections

Planting is an agricultural metaphor, and it expects growth and fruitfulness to occur in what is planted. The plant (i.e. that which the planter has planted) is expected to manifest 'plant-like' characteristics. So even though the word 'planter' is an agricultural metaphor, the word 'plant' is biological.

Biology as a science has progressed a long way since New Testament days, but surprisingly has discovered that the processes which define and distinguish any living thing from inert matter are quite simple. There are basically seven processes of life:

1. Movement
2. Respiration
3. Sensitivity
4. Growth
5. Reproduction
6. Excretion
7. Nutrition

These are always present in every living biological system, plant or animal, and when they work in consort they ensure growth and fruitfulness. When we apply these seven processes to the church, we give ourselves a checklist of life and health.

1. Movement

The people of God cannot be static. To live is to move. We must be constantly aware of the God-given challenge to move beyond what we know into what we do not, to reach out beyond where we already are and to recognize this as a vital sign of life. Whether the church has been planted recently or not, if it is alive it should be on the move.

Movement:

- occurs in response to stimuli;
- occurs at different speeds in different situations;
- uses up energy;
- is not sustainable for continuous periods.

When we plant – let us say a church – God may use different stimuli, sometimes even pressure or trial, but the result is intended to be the same: for movement to occur in the people of God. When movement takes place, it will occur at different speeds and sometimes with a different rhythm and pace. It will always use up energy and so we will have to rely on God to supply all that we need. Even though he is the supplier, movement, while necessary, will not be a continuous feature of our life. Whenever we plant, however, we should look for movement.

2. Respiration

The church is dependent on the breath of God. God's Spirit gives us life as he flows through us and among us. The Holy Spirit will ensure that a living church receives energy to convert into life-giving ministry.

Respiration:

- is a basic function of all life, occurring as a chemical reaction in every cell of every organism;
- takes place within specialized areas within each cell called mitochondria, nicknamed the 'power houses';

- requires the process of breathing;
- is a natural, automatic process which happens without conscious thought or effort;
- is constant;
- produces waste that needs to be exhaled;
- underpins most, if not all, other life processes.

Living in the presence of God's Spirit should be as natural as breathing. He will inspire life change and all other spiritual processes of life. We learn to do this best as we practise the disciplines of prayer and worship. A living church is a breathing church.

3. Sensitivity

A living church is also a sensitive church, able to respond to both God and people, the physical and spiritual environment.

In nature:

- sensitivity is the ability to respond to stimuli, the environment or other organisms;
- when sensitivity is increased or decreased it can be dangerous, or even fatal;
- sensitivity prompts movement;
- receptor cells are the main reason why an organism is able to respond to stimuli.

God gives particular gifts of prophecy and discernment to enable the church to hear him and respond to the spiritual environment, so that we can move away from danger and towards safety. He gives such gifts as pastoral care, mercy and hospitality, which enable us to respond with sensitivity to the needs of those around us. Such qualities mark out a living church.

4. Growth

If it is alive, it grows! If it does not grow, the forces of life are beginning to diminish. Growth is not a constant feature of anything that God has made – rest is also needed. Yet if a church does not grow, it will die.

The life process of growth:

- requires energy;
- is an increase in size and shape or numbers;
- is an automatic process if no inhibiting factors are operating;
- is non-linear (often exponential);
- has a ceiling defined by various factors.

The energy that God provides through spiritual respiration and nutrition ensures that the church is always able to grow. This will mean an increase in numbers, but numbers will only increase if the infrastructure also continues to grow (see Chapter 6). When a church ceases or slows down in growth, it is because inhibiting factors are beginning to supersede growth-promoting ones, but all churches will have a natural limit to the size to which they can grow. After this, only reproduction will continue life.

5. Reproduction

All animals have babies; all plants bear fruit; all Christians and churches should reproduce themselves. This is a spiritual necessity and a gospel imperative. If the church is healthy, it will reproduce.

In nature, reproduction:

- is the most important feature of all life processes;
- requires energy;
- is focused on producing healthy, strong, vital examples.

Jesus said that his disciples would bring glory to the Father by bearing much fruit. This is simple reproductive language. Multiplication is an unavoidable feature of a healthy spiritual life. In nature a species will tend to prevent the unhealthy and weaker members from reproducing. The strongest and most vital examples are the ones that predominate. Perhaps this is why God allows certain churches to multiply and prevents others from doing so? Perhaps this is one of the reasons why the churches of the developing world far exceed those of the Western world in their ability to reproduce?

6. Excretion

Although this is a subject rarely spoken of, it is an absolute necessity for life and health. This is true in both the physical and spiritual environments. All living things need to be able to remove toxic and unhelpful material from their systems.

Excretion:

- is basic to all life forms;
- is continuous but under voluntary control;
- produces waste products;
- includes recycling waste.

Confession and forgiveness removes the unhelpful and toxic barrier that exists between us and God. If it is not dealt with, it will cut us off from the Source of Life. This is true at both the individual and the corporate level, and so the challenge to repentance and accountability, the call to a holy life, must be heard in order for life and health to be maintained.

7. Nutrition

Everyone understands that we need food to thrive. All living things reach out for sustenance of some kind. The people of God are no exception. Jesus is the Bread of Life, the food that we need to prosper and grow. The Bible is the menu that describes what we are to take and receive.

As a life process, nutrition:

- is fundamental to life and health;
- is the taking in of substances to build the body, structures (skeleton), organs and tissues;
- is the fuel that produces the energy for all other life processes;
- requires the processes of movement and respiration.

One of the clearest needs of a healthy church is fuel for life. One of the greatest responsibilities of those who lead is the provision of wholesome, life-giving food. We must 'preach the Word . . . in season and out of season' (2 Timothy 4:2).

Conclusion

When we plant, we should monitor what has been done so that we can care for the church of God as God would want us to. These processes of life will perhaps give us some clues as to where we should start.

Are you . . .

Is your church (plant) . . .

- moving?
- respiring?
- sensitive?
- growing?
- reproducing?
- excreting waste?
- seeking nutrition?

5

Bridger

K IMPORTANT

I can remember the occasion well. I was seated in an old leather armchair in the study of a Cambridge vicar, overlooking the lawns of Jesus College. There were only two or three of us present. Somehow we had been invited to meet and listen to a church leader from Pakistan called Vinay Samuel. It was one of those life-changing moments, when someone else's story so impacts you that it becomes part of your story too.

Vinay told of how he and a small group of Christians from his church in Bangalore ventured into a shanty town populated by the poorest people in his city. It so happened that they arrived in the community at the same time as a Western missionary agency. The missionaries saw the squalor and immediately sent a major part of their team home to raise funds for a medical centre.

Vinay had a different strategy. He went to the elders of the community and asked them what it was they wanted God to do for them, and in what ways he and his group could help. The answer was unusual: they wanted a postbox, a place where they could post letters and send them to the outside world. Somewhat surprised, Vinay asked why it was that the elders wanted this when there were so many other obvious and pressing needs among this poor group of people. They said that if they had a postbox, then their community would have to become an officially recognized postal district. If they became a postal district, then they would legally exist as a community, which meant that the government authorities would not be allowed to send in bulldozers to systematically destroy their homes in the hope that they would find somewhere else to live.

Vinay and his team agreed to pray for this objective and to work together with the community leaders to influence the government to agree to their demands. They had no idea how hard such an apparently simple task would be. They were opposed and pilloried by government officials, persecuted and abused by police, but after two years of struggle – of letters, demonstrations and appeals – the elders' request was granted.

The Western missionaries built their medical centre, but found it difficult to convince the community to use it and even more difficult to gain a hearing for the gospel. Then the great day arrived. The builders came and set the postbox by the side of the road in the centre of the community. The elders and people celebrated enthusiastically, then they came to Vinay and said that they would love to hear about his God and the message that he had sent him and his team to deliver. Today that community is still poor, but it is now Christian.

For Vinay, the bridge-building exercise into another community and a different culture required risk, sacrifice and a commitment to listen, to understand and to communicate the gospel in ways that were appropriate for the particular community concerned. This remains the task of the church if all people are to hear the gospel.

The book of Revelation offers a vision of what the church will become:

> After this I looked and there before me was a great multitude that no-one could count, from every nation, tribe, people and language, standing before the throne and in front of the Lamb. They were wearing white robes and were holding palm branches in their hands. And they cried out in a loud voice: 'Salvation belongs to our God, who sits on the throne, and to the Lamb.' (Revelation 7:9–10)

John's vision of heaven and the destiny of humankind reveals the people of God – redeemed and united in their common praise of him – coming from the four corners of the globe and from every people group on the planet. This has always been God's plan for humanity, but for each tribe, tongue and nation to be reached it requires the people of God to leave the comfort of their own culture and reach out to one that is unfamiliar. Jesus our apostle has left the comfort and security of heaven and has crossed the most fundamental of divides, that which exists between God and people, heaven and earth. Having called his disciples to join him in the enterprise of the gospel, he does not excuse them from the challenge of the same kind of apostolic mission: to build bridges from what they know to what they do not know. 'But you will receive power when

the Holy Spirit comes on you, and you will be my witnesses in Jerusalem, and in all Judea and Samaria, and
to the ends of the earth' (Acts 1:8).

So the apostolic mission of the church is inaugurated
and one of the fundamental components of this work
is identified. To be apostolic means to build bridges
from one culture to the next. The disciples were called
to begin with Jerusalem, the capital of Israel and the
focus up to that point of God's redemptive activity in
history. From here – where the Spirit would be poured
out – the disciples were to go to all of Judea, which was
both a geographical and a cultural target group.
Geographically Judea was the area that surrounded
the city of Jerusalem, where many Jews in the time of
Jesus still lived, but the phrase 'all Judea' would also
have been understood by the disciples to refer to all the
Jews throughout the world. The Jews were a dispersed
group, but were still considered by both the rabbis and
the people to represent a single people group with the
same culture and worldview. To build bridges from
Jerusalem to Judea (and the Jewish people) simply
required accepting the necessities of travel, but to
reach the next group – the Samaritans – required much
more.

The Samaritans were despised, even hated, by the
Jews. The enmity between the two groups which had
developed over centuries was by now proverbial.
When Jesus wanted to identify the kind of person his
Jewish hearers would find it most difficult to connect
with and care for, he used a Samaritan in the parable of
the Good Samaritan. The Samaritans, though similar in
their beliefs to the Jews, were sufficiently different for

the rabbis and religious leaders of Israel to describe them as heretics – separated from the covenants of blessing and excluded from the heritage of the people of God. For a Jew even to talk to a Samaritan required a real miracle. For Jews to love Samaritans enough to risk their own lives to share God's message with them was unthinkable. Yet this is what Jesus required.

To reach out from Jerusalem to Judea necessitated that the disciples should learn how to travel with the message, and therefore required that they should operate in a lightweight and low-maintenance fashion. For them to reach beyond Judea to the Samaritans required that they should learn both the basics of cross-cultural communication and a reliance on God in an alien and often hostile environment. This meant a simplicity of speech and flexibility of operation far beyond the expectations of the average person, either then or now. If these steps from Jerusalem to Judea to Samaria were taken, however, then the journey to the ends of the earth was possible. Everything that needed to be learnt for such a challenge would have been encountered before this momentous step was made.

When the government of New South Wales wanted to build the Sydney Harbour Bridge, they looked for companies that could meet the specifications of such an enormous task. In its day it was the largest civil engineering project in the world, producing a bridge that still has the largest steel arch span ever constructed. Many tenders for the work were received, but finally Dorman Long of Middlesborough, England, were given the contract. They were one of the great bridge-building companies of the world and, interestingly, the bridge they built in England across the River Tyne at Newcastle served as a prototype for the much larger Sydney Harbour Bridge in Australia.

Although it was a shorter span, crossing the Tyne taught Dorman Long all they needed to learn for the greater and more challenging task of connecting both sides of Sydney Harbour. In similar fashion, the apostles leading the early church learned the principles of cross-cultural mission by making the progressive steps that Jesus had laid out. The span from Jerusalem to Judea helped them to learn what they needed to discover for the crossing into Samaria, and what they found there equipped them for the enormous leap towards the ends of the earth.

Having said this, however, the task was so large that they would not be able to attempt it without special help. Jesus told them to wait for God's empowering presence as the Holy Spirit came to fill them all and equip them to fulfil the call that he had given.

As if to underline God's intention and the destiny for the people of God, the Day of Pentecost was chosen to be the first day of cross-cultural communication in the church's history.

> Then how is it that each of us hears them in his own native language? Parthians, Medes and Elamites; residents of Mesopotamia, Judea and Cappadocia, Pontus and Asia, Phrygia and Pamphylia, Egypt and the parts of Libya near Cyrene; visitors from Rome (both Jews and converts to Judaism); Cretans and Arabs – we hear them declaring the wonders of God in our own tongues! (Acts 2:8–11)

On the day of its birth, the Holy Spirit supernaturally equipped the church to communicate with every part of the known world, proclaiming the good news of God's love in many different languages. Although the hearers were all Jews and so therefore shared the same cultural worldview as that of the disciples, they could have been in no doubt that the Holy Spirit was underlining the words of Jesus to reach out to the whole world and rely on him as they did so.

Yet this was a hazardous journey fraught with difficulties. The apostles and New Testament church learned slowly at first. Their apparent reluctance is often criticized by preachers and commentators, but we must remember that they were the first to attempt this task and so also the first to meet the obstacles. As such, they remain good models for us because their success was not easily achieved. Perhaps some examples from the first apostles will give us insight into how we should proceed today.

The Samaritans

Philip was an evangelist. He lived to talk. Until now, like most of the other followers of Jesus, he had lived and worked in and around Jerusalem. Philip was one of the seven people appointed by the apostles to oversee the administration of the Jerusalem church and, like his friend Stephen, he was extraordinarily gifted, moving in miraculous supernatural power. After Stephen's summary execution and the violent persecution that followed, Philip had been forced to leave and find safer havens elsewhere, along with most of the Jerusalem church. Philip went to Samaria (see Acts 8:4–5).

Having already been equipped by God as a communicator and given gifts of power with which to demonstrate the authenticity of his message (see Acts 8:6–7), Philip's work had proved successful. Yet even though he was equipped as he was, the work was incomplete because those who believed still did not experience the infilling of the Holy Spirit. Why was this? Did he lack something as an evangelist? I doubt it. It is more likely that the Lord wanted the apostles to be involved in pioneering the mission to the Samaritan people, building the cross-cultural bridges necessary for the wholly Jewish church to include within its membership those of Samaritan birth. And so, although the work began with Philip, the Lord would not allow it to be completed until the Twelve he had called to this mission were obedient.

Jesus made occasional contacts with Samaritans throughout his ministry. His main task was to reach 'the lost sheep of Israel' (Matthew 15:24), but his contacts with Samaritans and other Gentiles modelled what he wanted his disciples to do after his ascension.

We saw in Chapter 2 that as an apostolic bridger, Jesus:

- recognized the different needs of different cultures;
- communicated appropriately according to cultural needs;
- used his pioneering and planting gifts to establish a cross-cultural bridgehead;
- addressed cultural prejudices among his disciples so

that their eyes would be opened to the new bridging opportunity.

As they had been excluded, persecuted and despised by the Jews for so long, it is not surprising that God would send the leaders of the emerging church to 'lay hands' on them. The Samaritans knew that Jews would not touch them because they believed them to be unclean, yet here were God's anointed leaders touching them and praying for them, demonstrating that they were now one people.

With the outpouring of the Holy Spirit at the laying on of hands, the Samaritans could be convinced that the blessings of God were no longer denied to them. They were included. This demonstration of God's favour and acceptance was as important for the apostles as it was for the Samaritans. Although apparently reluctant, they could now not escape the conclusion that Jesus was fulfilling his prophecy of cross-cultural evangelism before their very eyes.

Philip continued with his cross-cultural exploits (witnessing to the Ethiopian Jewish proselyte in his chariot as he travelled across the Gaza desert), but it was not long before the apostles themselves were thrust into this next stage of mission.

Peter and Cornelius

One day, Peter was praying during the midday siesta on the roof of a friend's house in the coastal town of Joppa. As he prayed, the now famous vision unfolded before him – a bulging sheet held by its four corners by some invisible force was being lowered to the earth. In the sheet were pigs, vultures, snakes, lizards, crabs and lobsters – in fact everything that was forbidden as food. The sight must have been disgusting to any Jewish eye (and, quite frankly, not very palatable to anyone else either!). The unmistakable voice of God said, 'Kill and eat' (Acts 10:13). Peter was scandalized and could not obey, but the same voice from heaven told him not to reject anything that God had made. For emphasis, God gave this vision three times and then called Peter to take an extraordinary step of faith.

A God-fearing Roman centurion called Cornelius had, at the behest of an angel, sent servants to ask if Peter would come and instruct them. Peter, obedient to the voice from heaven telling him not to reject but to accept all that God had made, followed the men to this Gentile's home. As he spoke to the avid listeners, the Spirit of God interrupted his sermon and filled all those who were listening, causing them to speak in tongues. The Jewish believers who had come with Peter were amazed. Obviously this was an unexpected development in the unfolding mission of God.

Working by his Spirit, Jesus the apostle had been working in Peter the apostle. He had addressed his prejudices, established a bridgehead, communicated effectively through word and deed – sermon and spiritual power – and in this revealed that he recognized the particular needs of this new group in hearing the gospel. Although still a novice, Peter could see what the Lord was doing through him and was being discipled into this part of his apostolic calling – and no doubt he was reminded of the other occasions when the Lord had worked in that way.

In his explanation to the Jerusalem church, Peter said, 'If God gave them the same gift as he gave us, who believed in the Lord Jesus Christ, who was I to think that I could oppose God?' The church got the message. Their response was, 'So then, God has granted even the Gentiles repentance unto life' (Acts 11:17–18).

We may be surprised at the apparent reluctance of Peter and the others to reach out beyond the cultural confines of the Jewish people, but the experience of the church down the ages, and our experience still today, is that cross-cultural bridge-building – establishing new churches among different cultures – is among the most challenging and demanding of apostolic tasks. If it does not shake us to our core, we have probably not really done it!

What was certain was that the church would never be the same again. God's intention to bring all peoples into his kingdom was now well under way. The fundamental step had been taken. Now all cultures, every tribe, would hear the gospel in their own language. From this breakthrough, the apostle Paul took the mission one stage further and began to grapple with some of the great questions of cross-cultural communication.

Paul in Athens

Paul was alone. He had left his team behind and had to face the challenge of sharing the gospel in the world's cultural capital by himself. As we have seen in earlier chapters, working alone was not the normal pattern for apostolic ministry, but without any alternatives this time, Paul entered the fray.

As he wandered the streets and marketplaces, he noticed the idols on every street corner and the apparent devotion to many deities. Paul recognized the needs of these people. They were deeply religious, searching for meaning and hoping that a god of the Graeco-Roman pantheon would provide this for them. Through his walks, Paul also identified an important starting point for cross-cultural communication.

As he watched and listened, he learned how to speak. There was a shrine to an unknown god, revealing that these people were very keen to stay on the right side of any divinity that might have influence over their lives, but also revealing a desire to learn and discover more about the spiritual world which lay beyond their immediate grasp. Paul could begin with this mixture of religious fear and philosophical curiosity and speak about a god whom they had never encountered. Stepping out with all the courage that he could muster and speaking with undoubted apostolic authority, Paul began to address the people, telling them of the unknown god. His obvious ability and rhetorical skills came to the notice of the city fathers, who also wanted to hear his message. In this way he was able to pioneer a passage into this new and somewhat resistant culture and leave a few believers as the first foundation of the future church.

When we read the story of Paul in Athens in Acts 17, we notice that Paul as an apostolic bridge-builder uses the same principles and methodology developed and modelled by Jesus.

Like Jesus, he:

- recognized the needs of the Athenian culture;
- communicated appropriately;
- pioneered and planted a cross-cultural bridgehead;
- addressed cultural prejudices in his hearers.

The contemporary scene

Currently I lead a large church in one of the major urban centres of Britain. The membership of this church is made up largely of people under the age of 40, drawn from what sociologists have come to call Generation X. For many this has proved to be a culture highly resistant to the gospel. It is an extremely difficult mission field for the Western church to operate in, and yet our church has many hundreds of these very people. Developing a mission strategy to reach this group has been exciting and challenging and yet, frankly, for me it appears to be a natural and straight-forward matter. Others who visit our church cannot imagine how we can so successfully hold so many from a generation famously holding a post-Christian world-view, but for us it seems simple. Why is this? It is because God has taught us how to build big bridges by showing us first how to construct small ones.

My work among Generation X began 20 years ago when I was a children's worker in inner-city London. As those children grew older, I became a youth worker – not in the same place, but still among the same cul-tural group. As this group grew older, I became a student and young adult worker, and now I work among families as well as all the other age groups. Each of these stages was a major missiological challenge to me. God would not allow me to live with the meagre success I saw around me. I was prompted by the Holy Spirit to expect more. This meant learning to recognize the needs of this emerging culture, learning the appropriate models of communication, discovering how to apply pioneering and planting gifts to establish cross-cultural bridgeheads, and addressing my own cultural prejudices and those of the church around me. All of this meant that the internal obstacles within the life of the church, and the external challenges of the emerging culture, could be taken on stage by stage.

Building bridges is not an easy task and may take a lifetime to learn, but if we are to be obedient to the Great Commission and effective within our own generation, it is an enterprise with which we must engage.

Reflections

In Chapter 1 we said:

When we look at the adult membership of the church in the West, we find that in general there are three generations present in the church today. Sociologists and church-growth experts disagree on the finer points of classification, but for the sake of simplicity, the way I like to describe them is as follows:

1. The Builders (those over 60 years of age)
2. The Baby Boomers (40–60 years)
3. The Baby Busters (20–40 years)

The leadership, wealth and power of the church is found in the first two groups. The smallest group by far are the Baby Busters, often described as Generation X (or simply Xers). This is true both for mainline denominations and, to a lesser extent, for the new emerging networks and affiliations. This youngest generation most markedly reflects the rapid social change that has taken place. They are most definitely postmodern, post-industrial and 'urban' in their outlook.

In general terms, the Builders are more bookish than the other generations, have a greater appreciation and respect for the Bible, and recognize the needs of discipline, prudence and stewardship for a successful and healthy life. The Boomers, being the first generation to reap the benefits of widespread affluence, are the first generation to take the name 'consumer society'. In the West, the greater part of the economic machine has been geared to satisfy their physical and emotional needs. Although highly motivated, they are conscious of their own needs and are the first generation to develop a 'therapeutic society'. Generation Xers, born to busy, affluent Baby Boomers, have suffered the effects of increasing social change and stress. The majority have first-hand knowledge of family breakdown and so crave intimacy, community and belonging.

Although perhaps a little simplistic, it seems fair to say that the adult membership of society falls into these three generations. As well as this, however, they also fall into another three groups in relation to the church. These are as follows:

1. The churched (those who have attended church from infancy and are active members of their chosen Christian community)
2. The dechurched (those who, in the past, were part of a church but have now opted for a less active role, making only occasional visits, or no visits at all)
3. The unchurched (those who have never had any active involvement in a church or Christian organization)

If you were to plot the churched, dechurched and unchurched against the Builders, Boomers and Busters, you would discover that the Builders have the greatest proportion of churched people among them, the Boomers have the largest number of dechurched, and the Busters (or Generation Xers) have the largest number of unchurched.

This is not to say that examples of churched, dechurched and unchurched people cannot be found in all the generations, but the main point seems to hold. Understanding how to communicate with these various groups requires a good deal of sensitivity and perception. We need to recognize 'cultural givens' such as the prevalence and power of postmodernism, and 'tools for the job' such as careful observation. Only a few are mentioned in the tables following. Hopefully, however, these matrices will begin to provide some insight into the complexities of cross-cultural bridge-building.

	Builders	Boomers	Busters / Xers
Churched	Communicate using religious language	Speak to self-declared spiritual needs	Communicate how to encounter God at a deeper level
Dechurched	Assume religious background; answer questions that led to doubt	Offer non-religious, 'unchurchy' presentation of the gospel	Present Jesus as a spiritual answer to human need
Unchurched	Offer observations of life that lead to the 'right' questions being asked	Articulate gospel in terms of immediate concerns and recognized problems	Witness to what God is saying and doing among his people

	Builders	Boomers	Busters / Xers
Tools	King James Version of the Bible; well-known hymns, familiar liturgy	Modern language Bible; contemporary worship	Bible, music and liturgy used to create 'eclectic' worship
Givens	Appeal to right behaviour and decency	Need-oriented preaching and ministry	Narrative-based communication and visual culture

This is only a first attempt at defining the shape that communication should take, but nevertheless it is a starting point in building the necessary bridges to the different groups and cultures we are likely to encounter at any time.

As well as these cross-cultural realities, our open, multi-cultural, multi-ethnic world creates an almost bewildering kaleidoscope of overlapping groups, all of which need the message of salvation. A matrix something like the one provided above will begin to get the process of prayer and reflection started, so that we can begin to build bridges and reach every people group with the gospel.

6

Builder

Like Jesus, the New Testament apostles were builders.
They were used by God to establish and construct the
new community that he was calling into being. The
New Testament has several metaphors for this building
ministry, but the two most familiar ones focus on the
construction of a temple and on the growth of a human
body. In their writings, the apostles felt free to jump
from one metaphor to another, often using them inter-
changeably, but clearly some favoured one image more
than the others. In this chapter we will look at these two
images of the church found in the New Testament, both
used in the building ministry of the apostles. In doing
so we will also look at the two apostolic figures who
should by now have become quite familiar.

Peter the construction expert

Towards the end of his life, Peter wrote these words:

> As you come to him, the living Stone – rejected by men but
> chosen by God and precious to him – you also, like living

stones, are being built into a spiritual house to be a holy priesthood, offering spiritual sacrifices acceptable to God through Jesus Christ. (1 Peter 2:4–5)

Peter had spent many years leading and building up the people of God. As he writes to his beloved brothers and sisters, the image of building a temple – the place where God's presence was found – is central to his thoughts. God was somehow taking these persecuted, scattered Christians and constructing a 'place' for his presence to dwell. Jerusalem had been destroyed, the Temple razed to the ground and the Jewish Christians driven from their homeland. As well as this, Christians were suffering severe persecution throughout the Empire. This had been sanctioned by the Emperor himself and was being delivered by local government officials as well as by the general population. People were under severe pressure, feeling helpless and weak, scattered and broken, but Peter saw that God was doing something else. He was strengthening his people, building them up and gathering them into his purposes. Through their lives he was constructing a community in which his presence and glory would be known. For Jews, this presence and *shekinah* glory had previously been restricted to the Temple, hence the pre-eminent place of Jerusalem and the Temple Mount in the hearts of God's people. Peter was claiming that the presence and glory was just as real as it ever was, but its location was now found wherever the community of believers could be seen. They were, in a very real sense, 'the new temple' that God was building.

Why did Peter use this temple-building metaphor?

The answer may be that it was a familiar biblical model drawn from many parts of the Old Testament, sources on which both Peter and other New Testament apostles drew. Paul used the same analogy in the first part of his Corinthian correspondence. Perhaps Peter found it necessary, as 'apostle to the Jews', to use language with which his Jewish readers could identify. I think, however, that the reason for Peter's use of this metaphor is actually something far more significant.

Caesarea Philippi

Jesus had taken his disciples on retreat. He wanted to get away from the crowds, away from the spiritual conflict, and to spend quality time with the men who would lead his new movement. He took them from the populated areas around the Sea of Galilee into the open expanses of the region around Caesarea Philippi (see Matthew 16:13ff; Mark 8:27ff; Luke 9:18ff). With the breathtaking backdrop of the snow-capped Mount Hermon in the distance, Jesus led his disciples deeper into the things that he had for them. In typical rabbinical fashion, we find Jesus asking and answering questions. 'Who do people say I am?' Their answers ranged from 'an ancient prophet revisiting the earth' to 'a new teacher sent by God'. Pressing them further, he asked, 'But who do you say I am?' This was a moment of commitment, an opportunity for the disciples to nail their colours to the mast.

Peter was the first to respond. Way back at the beginning of this adventure, his brother Andrew had told him that Jesus was the Messiah. Everything that Peter had seen and heard since that time had confirmed this claim: the miraculous catch of fish, paralysed men walking, 5,000 people fed and, even more amazingly for him, Jesus and Peter walking on water. Yet somehow, Peter knew that Jesus being the Messiah was not enough to cover or explain all of his experience. In a way that was perhaps beyond Peter's ability to fathom, he sensed that Jesus was more than just the Messiah, greater than the long-awaited fulfilment of Old Testament prophecies. 'You are the Christ, the Son of the living God,' he said (Matthew 16:16).

> Jesus replied, 'Blessed are you, Simon son of Jonah, for this was not revealed to you by man, but by my Father in heaven. And I tell you that you are Peter, and on this rock I will build my church, and the gates of Hades will not overcome it. I will give you the keys of the kingdom of heaven; whatever you bind on earth will be bound in heaven, and whatever you loose on earth will be loosed in heaven.' (Matthew 16:17–19)

The response from Jesus was more than Peter had bargained for. Rather than just confirming or denying his claim, Jesus went on to make statements about Peter, his role and his destiny. Such a moment was surely etched into his heart and mind for ever. This, I believe, was the reason why the image of rocks, stones and buildings remained so prominent in Peter's teaching to the end of his life. Jesus had said that Peter was a 'little rock' (*petros*), and that upon the 'big rock' (*petra*) of his confession he would build his church. In saying this, Jesus was drawing on the rich tradition of Old Testament prophecy which made reference to the metaphors of rock and stone and the building of his kingdom. More than this, he was identifying the work that Peter would do for the rest of his life. Jesus was opening up the future to Peter.

This is one of the few times in the Gospels when Jesus speaks of building anything. It is also the first of only two mentions of the word 'church' by Jesus, so it is a tremendously significant passage. Jesus was saying that the revelation that he was the Messiah and the Son of God was the secure platform on which the new community – his gathered people – would be founded. He also said that in a very real sense he would be the architect of this new community. He, Jesus, would build it. There is little mention again of this metaphor in the teaching of Jesus. This one occasion was certainly enough for Peter to begin to piece together the picture of his own calling.

Jesus did make a few other references to the building metaphor. He would destroy the Temple and rebuild it in three days – and this would be used against him in his trial (see Matthew 26:61–3). He would call us to build our life on the 'rock' of his teaching. This same rock would be used to break resistance in men and women (see Luke 20:18). From the point of view of the disciples, however, what Jesus would soon reveal was even more significant: he would build his church, overseeing the construction, but *they* would put the blocks in place.

The Jerusalem church

After Pentecost, Peter functioned as the leader of the disciples and was the principal agent of God's work of reconstructing his people from the ruins of the Jewish nation. The new Christian community founded in Jerusalem after Pentecost bore all the marks of that established by Jesus among his twelve disciples. Jesus the apostolic builder had provided the basic structures for the newly emerging church, including the following:

- Teamwork
- Shared life
- Common resources
- Repeatable teaching
- Strategies for mission

The life of the Jerusalem church was in many ways just a large copy of the life of the twelve disciples (see Acts 2:42–7; 4:32–5).

The Twelve were the new leaders of God's people and were expected by God to carry on the work of Jesus by building the people into something that he wanted. Again we know that Peter understood this by the way he used Old Testament references when speaking to others. When he and John were dragged before the Sanhedrin to explain themselves for healing the crippled man at the Beautiful Gate, Peter quoted a familiar messianic text: 'He is "the stone you builders rejected, which has become the capstone".' Standing before the council, Peter changed the quotation slightly but decisively. Instead of the original reading, 'the stone *the* builders . . .' (Psalm 118:22), he says, 'the stone *you* builders . . .' (Acts 4:11). The priests and Sanhedrin, as leaders of God's people, were supposed to be builders, but they were bad builders who had rejected Jesus. As such they stood rejected and would be replaced by others whom God could use.

Tracing the development of the Jerusalem church, we can see that Peter and the other apostles understood the three basic elements of construction: foundations, framework and fabric.

Foundations

Jesus is the cornerstone. In masonry, great care was always taken over cutting the cornerstone. The angles, lines and dimensions had to be perfect because from this stone all the others would be aligned. The lines of the building would be defined by this stone. For this reason, the cornerstone was the largest and most important foundation stone used. If the cornerstone was right, the rest that were laid round it became a solid platform on which a building could be constructed. The cornerstone was the builder's set square.

It is quite easy to construct a dynamic picture from this beginning. If Jesus is the cornerstone, the first disciples who gathered round him were the rest of the foundation. Those who came after could therefore be confident that what they were being built into was both godly and good. This led to a great sense of security among the early believers.

Framework

A pattern emerges in the development of the church founded in Jerusalem – a simple infrastructure of differently sized groups, such as tends to emerge in the growth of any human community. This pattern had already found expression in Jewish society in the form of households, synagogues and Temple. The rabbis taught that each of these places of community expression was the location of God's blessing – in its own way.

The church, we are told, met together in homes and in larger groups, some of which were known by name. The 'Grecian Jews' and the 'Hebraic Jews' may have been names for congregations within the larger Jerusalem church, gathered on the basis of ethnic origin and common tongue (e.g. Acts 6:9). To what level these larger groups were organized is unclear, but it is not inconceivable to suggest that 'congregations' of this type began to emerge as the church grew. Added to these two emerging types of gatherings were even larger gatherings in Solomon's Portico at the Temple for teaching by the apostles (see Acts 2:46; 5:12).

What is known is that the creation of family groups and the collection of these families into clans of one kind or another is a basic, almost automatic, human response. In modern anthropology they have been called 'families', 'clans' and 'tribes' and have been represented in many ways in a multitude of different societies. Today the contemporary church growth movement would describe such groups as 'cells' (small groups), 'congregations' and 'celebrations'.

Fabric

The church was a spiritual building, not constructed with bricks and blocks but with people. This fact in some ways causes the metaphor to break down and requires Peter to refer in his writing to Christians as the 'living stones' and to balance the static image with more dynamic ones such as 'priesthood', 'nation' and 'chosen people'. As we read earlier:

> As you come to him, the living Stone – rejected by men but chosen by God and precious to him – you also, like living stones, are being built into a spiritual house to be a holy priesthood, offering spiritual sacrifices acceptable to God through Jesus Christ. (1 Peter 2:4–5)

The main point, however, remains and that is that everyone is needed, everyone is valuable, and all contribute to making what God has planned. We are all part of the building. We may not be the foundation, we may not be overseers of the framework, but everyone is part of the fabric.

These truths were worked into the life of Peter through his experiences in Jerusalem and no doubt through his later unrecorded experiences of apostolic work around the Roman Empire. And so we can see why, towards the end of his life, Peter 'the construction expert' called the church to be gathered as 'living stones' and built into the temple that God had designed – founded on the cornerstone of Jesus, built up by the teaching of apostolic leaders and crowned by the capstone, the piece in the arch that holds everything together, namely Jesus. He is the beginning and the end of the construction project, the first and the last.

Paul mirrored many of these thoughts, and used a similar analogy in his own writings.

You are . . . fellow-citizens with God's people and members of God's household, built on the foundation of the apostles and prophets, with Christ Jesus himself as the chief corner-stone. In him the whole building is joined together and rises to become a holy temple in the Lord. And in him you too are being built together to become a dwelling in which God lives by his Spirit. (Ephesians 2:19–22)

He even described himself as an 'expert builder' (1 Corinthians 3:10). Although it was important, however, this was not Paul's favourite image for the church. That was something quite different, and unique to him.

Paul the body builder

The surprising thing about Paul's use of this image is that it is not found as a metaphor of God's people in any clear sense within the Old Testament Scriptures. Paul was nothing if he was not a man of the Bible, so why would he use such an evocative image and, more to the point, where did he get it from? The simple answer is that he got it from the same place as Peter got his metaphor.

As a young Pharisee, Paul (known then as Saul) was zealous for truth and committed to the purity of the people of God. He was in the vanguard of those who persecuted the new and troubling sect of heretics who claimed that Jesus of Nazareth was the Messiah. He attempted to destroy everything that the twelve apos-tles had built up. 'But Saul began to destroy the church. Going from house to house, he dragged off men and women and put them in prison' (Acts 8:3).

Interestingly, Saul is seen to 'demolish' what had been built.[1] The way he did that was by attacking the framework and the fabric – the places of gathering (households) and the Christians themselves. What he did not know was that the cornerstone of the foundation was balanced over his head, and was about to crush him.

As we saw in Chapter 3, Paul's encounter with Jesus on the way to Damascus was the decisive moment in his life. It changed everything. Hearing the words of Jesus redefined his life and what he was about, but remember the important revelation about the church. In asking, 'Why do you persecute me?' Jesus was saying that when Paul persecuted Christians, he was actually inflicting pain on Jesus himself. He was revealing to Paul that his church was inextricably bound up with him, that the church was his 'body'.

Like Peter, Paul found his understanding of the church and his own calling defined by the personal revelation which had been given to him directly by Jesus. Peter was the rock, Jesus was calling him to build his church, so Peter's favourite image was of a temple. Paul had been a persecutor, hurting Jesus as he inflicted pain on the church, and therefore Paul's fundamental vision of the church was as the body of Christ. Probably unbeknown to Paul, as he lay on the dusty road dazed and blinded, he had been given an incredibly dynamic picture of the church which, when recorded in the New Testament, would provide many millions of Christians with a definitive vocabulary of community life.

---

[1] The actual meaning of the word translated 'destroy' in Acts 8:3 is 'demolish'.

On the road to Damascus, the seed of revelation was planted. It was watered by countless experiences of God's faithfulness and was confirmed by the patterns of life that Paul watched emerge in the churches in which he worked – first of all in the church in Antioch and then in the churches he planted, starting in Cyprus and continuing through Asia Minor and Europe.

As Paul reflected on these things and began to write letters to his churches, we see the development of the vision which had been planted in his heart all those years before.

> You are all sons of God through faith in Christ Jesus, for all of you who were baptised into Christ have clothed yourselves with Christ. There is neither Jew nor Greek, slave nor free, male nor female, for you are all one in Christ Jesus. If you belong to Christ, then you are Abraham's seed, and heirs according to the promise. (Galatians 3:26–9)

Writing from Corinth to the Christians in Rome, Paul began to introduce the idea of the body of Christ.

> Just as each of us has one body with many members, and these members do not all have the same function, so in Christ we who are many form one body, and each member belongs to all the others. (Romans 12:4–5)

He is feeling after something that he knows in his heart, but the expression has not yet reached full flower. Writing from Ephesus to the Corinthians, he takes the metaphor further:

> The body is a unit, though it is made up of many parts; and though all its parts are many, they form one body. So it is with

Christ. For we were all baptised by one Spirit into one body – whether Jews or Greeks, slave or free – and we were all given the one Spirit to drink. (1 Corinthians 12:12–13)

He has written much of this to the Romans, but as he reflects here on how the Christians in Corinth should interact with one another, encouraging the gifted participation of different members, the picture grows.

Now the body is not made up of one part but of many. If the foot should say, 'Because I am not a hand, I do not belong to the body,' it would not for that reason cease to be part of the body. And if the ear should say, 'Because I am not an eye, I do not belong to the body,' it would not for that reason cease to be part of the body. If the whole body were an eye, where would the sense of hearing be? If the whole body were an ear, where would the sense of smell be? (1 Corinthians 12:14–17)

Organism

Human bodies, like all biological organisms, reveal an interdependency between the different parts. This is something that biologists today fully understand and have studied at great depth, but Paul was taking the non-scientific, commonsense approach. He knew that everybody would understand what he was talking about because they all had a body themselves. So he goes on to say, 'The eye cannot say to the hand, "I don't need you!" And the head cannot say to the feet, "I don't need you!"' (1 Corinthians 12:21).

Paul was developing a picture of the church which has incredible depth and breadth. This is more than a picture or a simple illustration. Paul had discovered an allegory that could be applied to every part of the church and to every believer's experience within it.

He probably wrote 1 Corinthians during his time in Ephesus. Later, from Jerusalem, he wrote to the Ephesian Christians and to all the other churches of Asia Minor. By that time the image had grown into a fully rounded and comprehensive revelation.

> There is one body . . . But to each one of us grace has been given as Christ apportioned it . . . It was he who gave some to be apostles, some to be prophets, some to be evangelists, and some to be pastors and teachers . . . so that the body of Christ may be built up . . . we will in all things grow up into him who is the Head, that is, Christ. From him the whole body, joined and held together by every supporting ligament, grows and builds itself up in love, as each part does its work. (Ephesians 4:4, 7, 11–12, 15–16)

Paul witnessed his first revelation from the Damascus road grow into an image that was capable of conveying truth at both the general and the particular level. It still bears scrutiny today, revealing an astonishing grasp of both biology and theology. Paul was able to convey a sense of the church as organism and as organization. As an organism it was like all other living creations: it had movement, respiration, sensitivity, growth, reproduction, excretion and nutrition. Today biologists recognize these features as the seven fundamental processes of biological life (see Chapter 4).

Organization

As an organization, the church had three essential elements: source, structure and substance.

Source

Jesus is the head of the church.[2] As such, Christ is obviously in charge of his body and is able to give it directions as he sees fit. He is also the source, the one from whom the church gains its life and vitality, the one who is the starting point for all spiritual life.

Structure

Paul speaks of interconnected ligaments, and appears to describe apostles, prophets, evangelists, pastors and teachers as instrumental in building an infrastructure – a skeleton holding the body in place. The Greek word *katartismon* in verse 12, translated 'prepare', 'equip' or 'perfect', can be interpreted to mean 'the knitting together of bones'. The body of Christ needs an inner strength of ordered life and relationships that causes it to stand up. Without such an ordering of our lives, there would be no skeleton. Without a skeleton, the body would merely be a blob on the floor – not very attractive!

Substance

The 'stuff' of the church is Christians. Everyone is part of what God is building up and growing here on earth. All of us have a role, no one person is more important than another. This was vital for Paul and Peter to reiterate, because humans always tend to organize people in order of perceived importance. If this ordering were

---

[2] The word in Greek translated as 'head' in Ephesians 4:12 is *cephala*, which communicates both authority and source.

allowed, whole parts of the body of Christ would be left unused and unrecognized. God's plan is to use his whole body, with all the parts working harmoniously together to achieve the purpose of presenting Christ to the world.

Conclusion

As the first apostle, Jesus was the definitive builder. And as we have seen, this side of his apostolic work was replicated in the lives of the New Testament apostles. Each of the elements of Jesus' building ministry can be seen in the lives of the other apostles. The elements are worth repeating:

- Teamwork
- Shared life
- Common resources
- Repeatable teaching
- Strategies for mission

When brought together into the life of a single church community, the combination of these elements is explosive. In each of the three great church models in the Acts of the Apostles – Jerusalem, Antioch and Ephesus – these elements (explicitly or implicitly present) produce a remarkable dynamic which some have called 'concentration and spread'.[3] Each church gathered large numbers of people, and then sent out and

---

[3] Bob Hopkins and Richard White, *Enabling Church Planting* (CPAS, 1995), p. 5.

n scattered these same people into the mission of
Jesus. Peter was a principal agent in this dynamic
rhythm in the Jerusalem church, and Paul was a
product of this rhythm in Antioch and an agent in
Ephesus.[4]

Both Peter and Paul believed in building the church
of Jesus Christ. Both saw their own role as instrumental in this work. Both worked from the basis of calling
and revelation. If apostolic ministry is present today
within the church, as I believe it is, then the work of
building up the church remains. Apostles, along with
all others, must commit themselves to the aim of
growing a healthy, mature church. The vision is clear.
The tools are available. But how should it be done?

Reflections

A builder needs tried and tested materials so that a
foundation can be laid, a framework raised up and a
building fabricated. For me, the foundation of the
church is defined by biblical *vision* and *values*: the
vision is the kingdom and the values are those of grace.
The kingdom of God is the direction in which the
leader and the people of God are moving. We seek its
presence and fulfilment, and witness to its reality daily.
The grace of God reflects the generous giving heart of

---

[4] We know that Paul's work in Ephesus led to the planting of the
church in Colosse through Epaphras (see Colossians 1:7), but probably
this included the other churches of Asia Minor also mentioned in the
New Testament (see Colossians 4:16; Revelation 2:1–3:14).

God as he makes the gift of his Son, bringing the gift of salvation, bestowing the gift of the Spirit and all that we need for life and godliness. These define the breadth and depth of the platform upon which we can build.

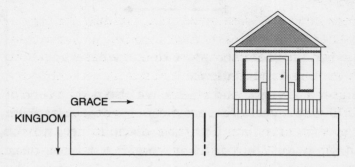

They also provide cross-hairs in our sights to keep us on target

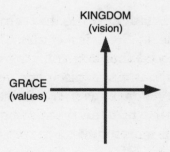

Focusing on the kingdom without a clear understanding of grace will cause us to tend towards striving.

Grace without a proper understanding of the kingdom will sometimes cause us to miss the challenge to move on.

STATIC ◄━━━━━━━━━━►

Together, kingdom and grace define what we need to lay down as a foundation.

As well as vision and values, we also need a *vocabulary*. Over the years, this has meant for me a rethinking of how to articulate Christian discipleship and the calling on the church. I have organized these basic truths around five geometric shapes: the circle, the semicircle, the triangle, the square and the pentagon.

1. Discipleship is taught using the learning *circle*. The word 'disciple' in Greek is *mathetes*. The easiest way to put this word into contemporary English is to translate it as 'learner'. A discipline of learning from Jesus is what he gave his first followers. The learning circle seeks to take this discipline of learning and apply it to our lives today.

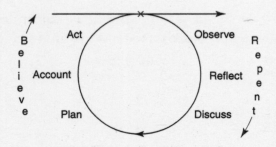

2. The rhythm of work and rest, abiding and fruitfulness is taught using the *semicircle*. Genesis tells us that human beings were created on the sixth day and that they were created to be fruitful. Yet having been created, their first experience after this was the Sabbath day, the day of rest. The semicircle teaches us how to work from rest and applies this to Jesus' teaching of abiding and bearing fruit.

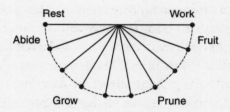

3. The balanced and holistic Christian life is taught using the *triangle*, which articulates the three fundamental relationships of life: the relationship to God – the upward dimension; the relationship towards the people of God – the inward dimension; and the relationship to the world – the outward dimension.

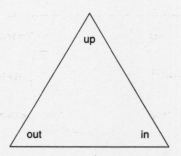

4. Servant leadership is taught by following Jesus as he adopts different styles of leadership with his disciples, and for this we use the leadership *square*. The first style of leadership is *directive*: 'Come, follow me' (Matthew 4:19). The second style of leadership is *coaching*, and is reflected in invitations such as, 'Take my yoke upon you and learn from me, for I am gentle and humble in heart, and you will find rest for your souls' (Matthew 11:29). The third kind of leadership is *pastoral*. It uses an approach based on consensus, which is particularly well illustrated by Jesus' comments at the Last Supper: 'I no longer call you servants . . . Instead, I have called you friends' (John 15:15). The fourth leadership style is *delegation*, which Jesus used in sending out his disciples to continue the work he had begun: 'Therefore go and make disciples of all nations, baptising them in the name of the Father and of the Son and of the Holy Spirit, and teaching them to obey everything I have commanded you' (Matthew 28:19–20).

5. Finding our place in the body of Christ means discovering our base ministry (see 'Reflections' in Chapters 7 and 8) and the *pentagon* is used to help people identify the fivefold ministries.

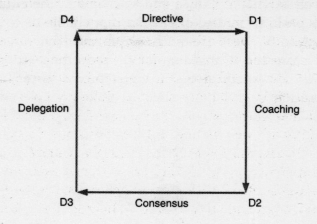

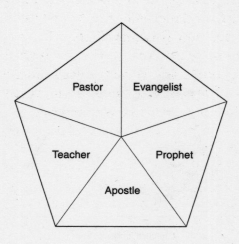

As well as vision, values and vocabulary, the church needs basic structures or *vehicles* that enable us to get from A to B. These are quite simple and have already been expressed in this chapter (in ascending order of size) as cell (small group), congregation (cluster) and celebration.

Small group

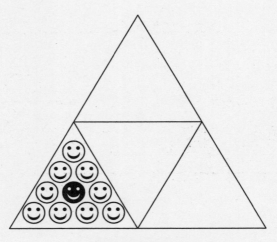

Cluster/Congregation

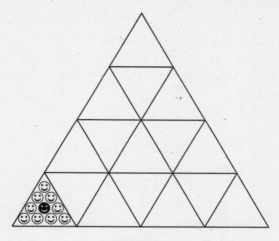

Celebration

Belonging

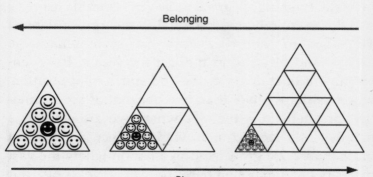

Size

7

Fivefold Ministries

Leaders become weary of hearing that church growth
in certain places is all down to the grace of God. 'Of
course it is,' they reply, 'but how does it work? What do
you do to respond to the grace of God?' Leaders want
practical teaching, clear examples, measurable results –
and this is entirely understandable and appropriate. St
Thomas's, the church I lead, has seen remarkable
growth and blessing in the last few years. In an environment of church decline and spiritual opposition,
where perhaps fewer than two per cent of the population of Sheffield – the city where we are set – is a
member of a local church, we have seen a church of
more than 2,000 grow. And in a nation where the vast
majority of church members are over 40 years old, our
church is made up largely of young people (75 per cent
are under 40). Of course, there are all kinds of reasons
for this that each express God's grace to us, but none is
more important than the release of the five ministries
spoken of in Ephesians 4.

The young leaders who have come through to positions of responsibility in these last few years, and who now staff the leadership team of St Thomas's, have a thorough understanding of the fivefold ministries. They know how to release and use these gifts for the continued growth and blessing of the church. For instance, one of our celebration leaders, during the time he was overseeing a small group in the church, understood that as a teacher he could impart truth and equip people to live in the freedom that truth brought, but it needed apostolic input for the group to grow beyond the smallness of a single group to the size and calling that God had for it. He brought in a recognized apostolic person from among the laity and, with my oversight and encouragement, released this person to do what came most naturally to him. Within a year, the small group had grown to what we call a 'cluster' – in this case, a gathering of four small groups. Soon after this another cluster grew. The remarkable growth was due to the interaction of different ministries being brought in at the right time and in the right way. This is precisely what Jesus had in mind when he returned to heaven and sent his grace to the church to function as his body in the world.

In this chapter, we will examine the five ministries of grace that Jesus gives to his church, and by doing this we will set the apostolic in its right biblical context. Apostles are only one part of a much more comprehensive picture.

But to each one of us grace has been given as Christ apportioned it. This is why it says: 'When he ascended on high, he led captives in his train and gave gifts to men.' (What does 'he ascended' mean except that he also descended to the lower, earthly regions? He who descended is the very one who ascended higher than all the heavens, in order to fill the whole universe.) It was he who gave some to be apostles, some to be prophets, some to be evangelists, and some to be pastors and teachers, to prepare God's people for works of service, so that the body of Christ may be built up until we all reach unity in the faith and in the knowledge of the Son of God and become mature, attaining to the whole measure of the fullness of Christ. (Ephesians 4:7–13)

Thousands of writers have written millions of words about these verses. So much teaching and material has been produced that it seems unnecessary to do any more: surely everything of importance that can be said has already been said?

Nonetheless, we must look again at this vital New Testament scripture for at least two reasons. First, even though so much has been written, no account of apostleship can be offered without some reference to this key text. And second, having reviewed much of what is taught about apostleship and the other ministries from this text, I have become convinced that the 'mainstream' charismatic and evangelical interpretations are wrong!

I realize that this seems somewhat bold, but it is not intended to be dismissive of all that has gone before. It is offered with the utmost respect, and after extensive study and reflection. I believe that Ephesians 4 teaches that there are five ministries and that every member of the church has been given one of them. In other words, everyone who is a Christian is an apostle, or a prophet, or an evangelist, or a teacher, or a pastor.

I have come to this position for two reasons. The first is that the text itself seems to suggest such an understanding. The second is that, as I have applied this teaching to the people in the churches that I have led, I have seen a remarkable release of life, growth and spiritual power. These two reasons represent the two horizons of biblical interpretation. The first horizon is an understanding of what the text actually says. The second horizon is the effect of the word as it is applied to our contemporary context. Understanding the text is one thing, working it out in our contemporary context is another. My study of the Bible and my experience of daily ministry convince me that a fresh interpretation is called for. Without presenting all the different positions and approaches (which would require far more space than is available in this book), I intend simply to offer my own interpretation of the text and allow you to make up your own mind.

Paul's letters are usually divided into two halves. The first half deals with theory, the second with practice. Thus the first two or three chapters of Ephesians deal with theory, some of which is quite complex. This is not irrelevant, intellectual theorizing, but theological and philosophical arguments that provide a secure platform for the rest of what Paul wants to say. In the fourth chapter, Paul moves on to application. He uses the metaphor of the body of Christ for the church, which we looked at in the last chapter. This picture was the dynamic vision of life and growth that Paul had for the church. It is worth taking another look at Paul's words here.

But to each one of us grace has been given as Christ apportioned it. This is why it says: 'When he ascended on high, he led captives in his train and gave gifts to men.' . . . It was he who gave some to be apostles, some to be prophets, some to be evangelists, and some to be pastors and teachers, to prepare God's people for works of service, so that the body of Christ may be built up until we all reach unity in the faith and in the knowledge of the Son of God and become mature, attaining to the whole measure of the fullness of Christ.

You may have noticed that I have left out verses 9 and 10. I have done this so that we can recognize the flow of Paul's thinking. Paul has moved from his theoretical to his practical section, but he finds it too tempting to drop in a few extra theological nuggets! When I did maths at school, I learned that you always deal with the brackets first. That is a helpful principle to apply to Paul's letters, because he often puts things in parentheses which are supplementary rather than central to his main point. The words inside these brackets are all about the incarnation and ascension of Christ. He wants to show that, because Christ has come to earth, carried our sin to hell and ascended into heaven, he is able to offer the gifts of heaven to human beings even though they are still on earth. This is a supplementary thought. To understand Paul's central thought, we need to read verse 11 as if it follows directly on from verses 7 and 8.

Paul says, 'But to each one of us grace has been given as Christ apportioned it.' 'Each one' refers to every member of the body of Christ. The body has a unity that Paul underlines in the first few verses of the chapter:

'. . . keep the unity . . . There is one body' (Ephesians 4:3–4). Within the unity, however, there is diversity. Each one of us, although part of the whole, has a different role and responsibility, and this diversity falls into five parts. Everyone has received this grace: some to be apostles, some to be prophets, some to be evangelists, some to be pastors and some to be teachers.

These ministries are a gift from God by his grace. Grace is God's self-giving initiative to human beings. The gift of love and forgiveness, the gift of holiness and sanctification, the gift of empowering and equipping – all are expressions of grace. In the case of Ephesians 4, Paul is dealing with the grace of God to empower and equip for service. 'To each one of us grace has been given . . .'

This means that every member of the church is one of the five ministries mentioned in verse 11. When I first saw this, I frankly could not believe it. Then I thought, if this is true, how does it work? How can I teach it? How does it fit with the other passages on spiritual gifts in the New Testament?

The first thing I discovered was that Paul was not necessarily addressing the same problems in all his letters. Obviously his target audience was different, but so was the truth he was seeking to convey: 1 Corinthians, Romans and Ephesians tackle different issues and so teach different things.

For instance, a careful reading of Corinthians would reveal that there were several problems that Paul was seeking to address:

- The fact that the Corinthian church had become self-focused

- Personal 'needs'
- Personal spirituality
- Individual gifting
- Personal preference
- Individual freedom

These needs manifested themselves in a church where everyone concerned themselves with their own 'spiritual high', leading to selfish behaviour and chaotic gatherings. To this situation, Paul wrote about unity (1 Corinthians 1:10), serving one another (1:33), purity over personal desire (chapters 6 and 7), and submitting to the Holy Spirit in worship (12:12–20).

When Paul was writing to Rome, however, he was addressing a quite different situation (see Romans 16:3). For a start, it was not a church that he had planted, but one about which he undoubtedly had lots of information. Priscilla and Aquila, well-known members and probably leaders of this church, were partners with Paul in ministry and would undoubtedly have revealed many of its 'secrets' to him (see Acts 18:2). This was a church that was struggling with ethnic divisions. The Jews and Gentiles within the congregation were not really functioning as a single church. Some of this was to do with the fact that they were struggling to work out how to apply the teaching of the Old Testament Scriptures to their lives; some of it was probably just old-fashioned racism. Paul hoped to visit them soon and so introduce the ministry they could expect from him.

Ephesians is different again. For a start, just about every New Testament scholar recognizes that this letter was not addressed to Ephesus exclusively, but was written as a general letter to the churches of Asia Minor, of which Ephesus was the principal one. Some of the evidence for this is found in the fact that during the early centuries of the Christian era, there appears to have been more than one copy of the letter we know as Ephesians. These copies appear to have been addressed to different churches in Asia Minor. Tertullian quotes from Ephesians and calls it 'The Letter to the Laodiceans', which is probably what Paul is referring to in Colossians when he suggests that the Christians there should read this letter (see Colossians 4:16). It is perhaps for this reason that, unlike Paul's other New Testament letters, Ephesians contains no personal greetings.

Ephesians was written as a 'round robin' letter. Careful reading reveals that Paul is concerned to offer teaching that has general application to all Christians. The teaching that he is most interested to share concerns what the church is, and how it should function. Interestingly, one of Paul's team planted a church among the Colossians in Asia Minor while he was in Ephesus (see Colossians 1:7). When this church experienced particular problems and difficulties, Paul used many of the insights he had gained in Ephesus and applied them to the issues arising in the Colossian church. This is why Colossians appears so similar to Ephesians and yet reads as quite a different letter.

The 'gift' passages

Each of these letters – Romans, 1 Corinthians, Ephesians – was addressed to a different situation and talked about different things. I am sure that Paul never intended the various lists of spiritual gifts to be somehow cobbled together. Connecting them is like comparing apples and oranges. If the various lists of gifts were meant to be joined as one, you have to ask, why are they not exhaustive? They do not include such things as worship-leading or intercession, yet these definitely seem to be spiritual gifts.

In each passage on spiritual gifts, we need to look for the word that unlocks the right interpretation. For instance, in the Ephesians text the key word is 'apportioned'. We will look at this in more detail later, but there are other passages we ought to look at first.

Corinthians

> Now about spiritual gifts, brothers, I do not want you to be ignorant. You know that when you were pagans, somehow or other you were influenced and led astray to mute idols. Therefore I tell you that no-one who is speaking by the Spirit of God says, 'Jesus be cursed,' and no-one can say, 'Jesus is Lord,' except by the Holy Spirit. There are different kinds of gifts, but the same Spirit. There are different kinds of service, but the same Lord. There are different kinds of working, but the same God works all of them in all men. Now to each one the manifestation of the Spirit is given for the common good. (1 Corinthians 12:1–7)

In this passage, the key word is 'manifestation' – *phanerosis* (1 Corinthians 12:7). It means the 'revelation' or 'enlightening' that God brings. 'Manifestation', the English word used to translate the Greek, is a word with a Latin origin that means 'the dancing hand'.

In 1 Corinthians 10–14, the context is the church's

worship time: Paul used the phrase 'when you come together' several times (see 1 Corinthians 11:18, 20, 33–34; 14:26). He wanted to teach them that when they came together something wonderful happened – *phanerosis* – God came and shone his light on different people within the worship in different ways. In a time of worship, the hand of the Spirit dances over the congregation, resting on whoever he wishes to give a particular gift to.

> To one there is given through the Spirit the message of wisdom, to another the message of knowledge by means of the same Spirit, to another faith by the same Spirit, to another gifts of healing by that one Spirit, to another miraculous powers, to another prophecy, to another distinguishing between spirits, to another speaking in different kinds of tongues, and to still another the interpretation of tongues. All these are the work of one and the same Spirit, and he gives them to each one, just as he determines. (1 Corinthians 12:8–11)

We cannot take from this text the idea that we only have one gift. The context, remember, is worship. We can receive a gift of the Spirit in worship, if we are open, because his hand can rest on us and manifest his presence in our lives in words of wisdom, knowledge, interpretation, prophecy, healing, tongues, etc. Within the gathered company, the church can receive all the gifts, and if we are prepared to wait on the Spirit, we may receive any of them. The key is that the Holy Spirit is within you and he is in charge of the worship time.

When a person receives the Spirit of God, he has access to the whole toolkit. The tools are manifest according to his will and purpose and according to our surrender and openness to him. The gifts are simply the evidence of his presence. If he is in our heart, we can manifest any of these gifts.

Romans

> Therefore, I urge you, brothers, in view of God's mercy, to offer your bodies as living sacrifices, holy and pleasing to God – this is your spiritual act of worship. Do not conform any longer to the pattern of this world, but be transformed by the renewing of your mind. Then you will be able to test and approve what God's will is – his good, pleasing and perfect will. For by the grace given me I say to every one of you: Do not think of yourself more highly than you ought, but rather think of yourself with sober judgment, in accordance with the measure of faith God has given you. Just as each of us has one body with many members, and these members do not all have the same function, so in Christ we who are many form one body, and each member belongs to all the others. We have different gifts, according to the grace given us. If a man's gift is prophesying, let him use it in proportion to his faith. If it is serving, let him serve; if it is teaching, let him teach; if it is encouraging, let him encourage; if it is contributing to the needs of others, let him give generously; if it is leadership, let him govern diligently; if it is showing mercy, let him do it cheerfully. (Romans 12:1–8)

This passage speaks about being 'living sacrifices' and being able to give of ourselves to God in a completely sacrificial way. The context here is different. Paul is talking about the readiness of Christians to serve. The word 'serve' is a continuous action, not just an event that we choose to do by surrendering ourselves to the will of God. The key word that helps us to interpret this passage is 'function' in verse 4 (Greek *praxis*). Paul is wanting to teach how Christians committed to a life-style of service can have different long-term functions within the body.

A fresh look at Ephesians 4

When he was writing Ephesians, Paul wanted to address all the churches of Asia Minor. He wanted to present a comprehensive theology of the church, and so we have teaching here that, although consistent with the rest of the New Testament, is found nowhere else. The two most important things about this text if we are to understand it are that (1) every believer receives one of the five ministries, and (2) each believer receives a different proportion of the gift than others.

Again, we need to understand the words Paul uses. The key words connected to this passage are 'grace', 'apportion', 'prepare', 'apostle', 'prophet', 'evangelist', 'pastor' and 'teacher'. Grace, God's self-giving initiative, is something we have already looked at, so let us take a look now at the idea of apportionment or measure (v. 7). Christ is delivering portions of grace which, when received by the believer, impart one of the fivefold ministries at some level of anointing.

Measure The translators of this text have attempted to convey the sense of what Paul is saying. Nonetheless, if they do not expect, or have not experienced, what Paul means, they may not be able to offer an adequate translation. In the original text, the word 'apportioned' (*metron*) is set against the words *doreas* and *dokein*, which in most translations are rendered as 'gift' and 'to give'. This is confusing, given that the sentence also includes the word *charis*, which is translated as 'grace' but also means 'gift'. The translators of the NIV do not fully translate this combination of words and their literal meanings, which means that they are able to come to the conclusions they do. I believe, however, that all the words should be translated if they are in the text, and when the two words for 'gift' in this passage are taken together along with *metron* (or measure), it would suggest that there may be different proportions of the ministries given to the church. A rough translation of verse 7 might be: 'Grace was given according to the measure of the gift of Christ.' This is very close to that rendered by the RSV.

Compare this with the NIV translation: 'But to each one of us grace has been given as Christ apportioned it.' The alternative translation would appear to me to take seriously all that Paul wanted to say, as well as begin to convey what he means: i.e. that there are different proportions of the ministries in the church. There may be lots of pastors and teachers, but fewer evangelists, prophets and apostles. Certainly this would seem to be true. There would not appear to be as many apostles as there are pastors. Also, and just as importantly, this combination of words seems to indicate a differentiation in the amount of anointing or empowering any individual receives for a particular ministry. Some are clearly more anointed than others, and this is what Paul is trying to convey.

One way that I have personally visualized this teaching is to imagine slices of cake, all of which are the same shape but some of which are thicker than others. This allows me to recognize that different people are called into an apostolic ministry, but some have a greater anointing than others.

Another picture that you might use is Jesus handing out tools: five different kinds – hammers, screwdrivers, saws, pliers, spanners. Within each category, the tool is the same, but one may be larger than another, with a different specification. You can have hammers that are useful for knocking in panel pins, and ones that can drive home a six-inch nail. The same might be said of the other tools.

Prepare 'Prepare' (Greek *katartismon*) is also translated 'equip' or 'perfect'. This word is a vital part of what Paul is saying. The ministries are intended to produce the effect for which God is looking. The church is Jesus to the world (his body), but it is made up of imperfect and inadequate members. As such it needs to grow in its ability to present the whole ministry of Christ. The Lord has seen fit to ensure that this will be achieved by him working through each member affecting all the others. Each Christian is a recipient of grace and becomes a channel or instrument of grace to everyone else.

Martyn Lloyd-Jones believed that this word *katartismon* was a medical term that spoke of the 'knitting together of bones': as the ministries are released and developed, the unseen infrastructure (skeleton) of the church causes it to stand tall, until 'we all reach unity in the faith and in the knowledge of the Son of God and become mature, attaining to the whole measure of the fullness of Christ' (Ephesians 4:13).

As we learn to communicate among ourselves – 'speaking the truth in love' (Ephesians 4:15) – the structure (skeleton) becomes mobile and flexible as responsiveness increases. The spiritual sinews connecting us together begin to work properly: 'From him the whole body, joined and held together by every supporting ligament, grows and builds itself up in love, as each part does its work' (Ephesians 4:16).

The other words of importance in this text are the ministry gifts themselves:

- Apostle – *apostolos*, one who is sent out
- Prophet – *prophetes*, one who hears and speaks on God's behalf
- Evangelist – *euanggelistes*, one who brings good news
- Pastor – *poimen*, one who shepherds God's people
- Teacher – *didaskalos*, one who holds out God's truth for people to receive

Putting all this together

God has imparted his empowering gift of grace to his whole church in five ways. These five ways are his chosen channels of grace to the church and through the church. All are included, none is left out. Relative to one another, some may have a greater impartation – more anointing than others – but all are one of the five ministries.

In Chapter 2 we saw that Jesus is the model and originator of all five ministries. As 'Jesus to the world', his body the church reveals his whole ministry in all five expressions of grace. We are all included in the continuing ministry of Christ to the world. By this, Christ gathers up all his redeemed people, gifts them and empowers them, and uses each one in a marvellous, interwoven tapestry of grace that displays his image to the world.

Reflections

Gift and ministry questionnaires can be dangerous things! We sometimes forget that only God can truly reveal his gift and call on our life, and we tend to set too much store by these kinds of exercises. Having said that, however, I hope you find this fivefold ministry questionnaire helpful.

Answer the questions *as quickly and as honestly as possible*. This often produces the most accurate results. Please remember that the results of this questionnaire are merely a slice in time, an attempted snapshot of your life right now. Hopefully it will help you to confirm both the base that you suspect you have and the phase in which you think you may currently be. 'Base' and 'phase' are usually represented by your two highest scores respectively. However, if you are a mature Christian who has already been through several cycles of phase ministry, you may have a high score for everything – but hopefully there will be sufficient variance to provide an indicator.

Have fun, and if it all goes wrong, try not to judge me too harshly!

Fivefold ministries questionnaire

Read through the statements and decide as honestly as you can whether you strongly agree, agree or disagree, and tick the appropriate box. Do not linger on each item, as your first thought is likely to represent the most accurate response.

Item no.		often	some-times	rarely
1	I remember names or at least where I first met someone			
2	I have expressed my feelings about God as pictures or analogies			
3	My ability to present Scripture clearly and accurately has been commented on			
4	I can be counted on to contribute original ideas			
5	I find myself talking about my faith to the people I meet			
6	I get frustrated when I feel I'm not experiencing 'new' things as a Christian			
7	When I communicate biblical truths to others I see resulting changes in knowledge, attitudes, values or conduct			
8	I share what knowledge I have with others			
9	I have an urge to share thoughts with people that I felt when I prayed and I have been told they meant something or were relevant to the person's current situation			
10	I get upset at other people's difficulties and problems even if I haven't experienced them myself			

11	I have a strong sense of what God wants to say to people in response to a particular situation			
12	I enjoy studying the Scriptures and find that I get fresh insights that people find interesting and helpful			
13	When reading the Bible I am more able to grasp the wider picture or message than the specific details			
14	I like to share what I believe			
15	I have been successful in developing Christian discipline in others			
16	I'll try things out if it will encourage others to do the same			
17	I am quick to help when help is needed and often do things which I see need to be done without even being asked			
18	I have been able to spot a 'person of peace' who is ready to receive a word from God and have seen a positive response			
19	I have a clear vision and others have said that they feel confident to go along with me			
20	I try explaining things in different ways if people are finding a concept difficult to grasp or understand			
21	I think before I speak			

Item no.		often	some-times	rarely
22	I really fear that people I know will not be saved			
23	I like to be clear and decisive when speaking about what I believe God has said to me			
24	I am by no means an expert on Scripture, but I can grasp the point of a passage quite quickly			
25	I get frustrated and even depressed at the lack of faith or understanding of others around me			
26	People tell me that the things I say often help them to try new things for God			
27	I am interested in living and working overseas or among people from a different culture.			
28	I am good at listening and taking in what people say			
29	I have contrived situations so that non-Christians are prompted to ask spiritual questions			
30	I have helped fellow believers by guiding them to relevant portions of the Bible			
31	I get excited when I discover new understanding, insights and applications of God's word			

32	I have reminded people of the foundations of their faith					
33	Despite not enjoying the nitty-gritty details of leadership, I still often end up leading things					
34	People have told me that I have helped them be restored to the Christian community					
35	I feel that I know exactly what God wants to do in ministry at a specific point in time					
36	I dig out information and passages to explain a concept					
37	I mix easily with a wide variety of people without having to try to be one of them					
38	I have a deep concern to encourage people towards spiritual growth and achievement					
39	I try to think of different ways of expressing the truth of the gospel					
40	Friends ask me to help clarify a situation or scripture					
41	I am quite persuasive when encouraging people to examine their spiritual motives					
42	I empathize with those who are hurting or broken and can support them through their pain to wholeness					

Item no.		often	some-times	rarely
43	When in a group, I am the one others often look to for vision and direction			
44	I enjoy being with non-believers because of my desire to win them to Christ			
45	I will see a job through to the end so that no one has to pick up the pieces after me			
46	My prayers surprise me with their clarity and unexpected direction			
47	People comment that they remember what I tell them about God			
48	I *expect* opportunities for witnessing to arise rather than react in surprise when they occur			
49	I desire the gift of healing in greater measure (that the Lord would heal others through me)			
50	The things I say in a spiritual context make people feel uncomfortable			
51	I have enjoyed relating to a certain group of people over a period of time, sharing personally in their successes and their failures			
52	People have told me that I have helped them learn biblical truth in a meaningful way			
53	I have led someone to a decision for salvation through faith in Christ			

54	God has enabled me to reveal specific things which have happened or meant something at a later date				
55	There have been times when I felt sure I knew God's specific will for the future growth of his work, even when others have not been so sure				
56	People have told me that I have communicated timely words or pictures which must have come directly from the Lord				
57	People call on me to help those who are less fortunate				
58	I get great satisfaction from studying the Bible and sharing my insights with others				
59	Others have suggested that I am a person of unusual vision				
60	Non-Christians have noted that they feel comfortable when they are around me, and that I have a positive effect on them towards developing a faith in Christ				
61	I am willing to challenge or confront people in order to help them mature				
62	I regularly need to get space alone or long periods of time out to reflect, pray and think				
63	I have just suddenly known something about someone				
64	I enjoy taking notes when someone is speaking and pay close attention to the details of what they are saying				

Item no.		often	some-times	rarely
65	I am faithful in providing support, care and nurture for others over long periods of time, even when others have stopped			
66	I enjoy mentoring individuals			
67	I enjoy relating stories and sharing my experiences			
68	I enjoy coming up with new and original ideas, dreaming big and thinking about visions for the future			
69	I find non-Christians ask me questions about my faith in Christ, and my church involvement			
70	I can accurately assess a person based on first impressions and know instinctively when something is not quite right			
71	I like to provide a safe and comfortable environment where people feel they are welcome, that they belong, are listened to and cared for			
72	I would like to start a church or a new ministry in an area which is not catered for at present			
73	I have a heart to share my faith and to pray for those in my work and neighbourhood who do not attend church			
74	When I hear about situations of need I feel burdened to pray			

75	I like to help churches, organizations, groups and leaders become more efficient and often find myself thinking about how things function			
76	I enjoy spending time studying Scripture and prefer to do so systematically			
77	I look for opportunities to socialize and to build relationships with non-Christians			
78	People come to me to ask me my opinions on particular parts of the Bible or to answer their queries			
79	I find that people trust me and come to me regularly, wanting to chat and looking for my advice, prayers and help			
80	I can clarify goals, develop strategies, and use resources effectively to accomplish tasks			

Now transfer your answers to the score sheet on the facing page and add up your totals.

- Place a tick against each item number for which you answered 'often' or 'sometimes' (the 'rarely' answers are not counted, but you may wish to use the shaded column for 'rarely' to keep tabs on which answers you have transferred from the question sheet).
- Note that some questions occur more than once in the columns on the score sheet.
- Finally, add up the number of 'often' ticks, double the answer and add to the number of ticks for 'sometimes'.
- Please refer to the appendix on page 220 to discover which of the five ministries you are currently operating in.

Remember this is only a snapshot. If you want to use the questionnaire to provide a more accurate picture, you will have to use it on several occasions in the future and keep your results to compare. I think that if you answered the questions two or three times a year for two or three years, you would begin to get a clear picture both of your base ministry and of the phases you were most regularly visiting.

In the next chapter we will look more closely at the notions of base and phase ministries.

Item No.	A Often	B Some-times	C Rarely
1			
10			
17			
21			
28			
30			
34			
42			
45			
49			
51			
57			
53			
60			
65			
66			
71			
79			

Totals: A ☐ B ☐ C ☐
Multiply total in A by 2 = D ☐
Grand total (B + D) = ☐

Item No.	A Often	B Some-times	C Rarely
2			
9			
11			
23			
25			
31			
35			
41			
46			
50			
54			
56			
27			
55			
62			
63			
70			
74			

Totals: A ☐ B ☐ C ☐
Multiply total in A by 2 = D ☐
Grand total (B + D) = ☐

Item No.	A Often	B Some-times	C Rarely
3			
7			
8			
12			
15			
20			
24			
36			
40			
47			
52			
58			
21			
39			
64			
67			
76			
78			

Totals: A ☐ B ☐ C ☐
Multiply total in A by 2 = D ☐
Grand total (B + D) = ☐

Item No.	A Often	B Some-times	C Rarely
5			
14			
18			
22			
29			
32			
37			
39			
44			
48			
53			
60			
1			
51			
61			
69			
73			
77			

Totals: A ☐ B ☐ C ☐
Multiply total in A by 2 = D ☐
Grand total (B + D) = ☐

Item No.	A Often	B Some-times	C Rarely
4			
6			
13			
16			
19			
26			
27			
33			
38			
43			
55			
59			
32			
11			
68			
72			
75			
80			

Totals: A ☐ B ☐ C ☐
Multiply total in A by 2 = D ☐
Grand total (B + D) = ☐

8

Base and Phase Ministries

I became a Christian by reading the Bible. As a 16-year-old interested in the world and eager for answers to the big questions of life, I could often be found in deep discussion or hot debate, struggling with what seemed to me to be issues of life and death. Fortunately for me, the school I attended had a large number of Christians on the staff. They were only too eager to take up the challenge of debate. I can remember one occasion very well: a substitute RE teacher called Mrs Demarese (who, unknown to me, had also been a missionary to Africa) was discussing the subject of the second coming of Christ. I can remember being shocked by the thought that many people actually believed that Christ was returning, and not as a child or a teacher, but as a king.

As always, I was ready to take up the challenge of debate, but found myself bettered at every turn. Finally, at the end of the lesson and with a good deal of exasperation, I told the teacher that I thought it was unfair that she had so much more material at her fingertips and that I needed a chance to be similarly equipped. She offered me a Bible – one of the new translations – which I readily accepted, took away and began to read. The head of the RE department got to hear about the situation and offered to replace my dog-eared school edition for a rather nice study version, complete with photos of contemporary-looking young people on the front cover and guides to reading within. During the summer holidays, I read large portions of both the Old and the New Testament and became convinced, not only of the existence of God, but of the claims of Christ. I began attending a local church and soon found myself being discipled by the young assistant minister.

Round about this time, I can remember lying in bed at night enjoying the new sense of peace that I had found, feeling a growing sense of excitement about the future, and asking God directly what I was supposed to do with my life. I fully expected God to answer, and he did. (It was not until later life that the cynicism of those around me challenged this expectation.) God said that I was to be a missionary and that this calling was for the rest of my life. I now realize that God was using language I could understand since I had no church background and little biblical vocabulary at my disposal. By 'missionary' I understood that he was calling me to be one who was 'sent out'. Of course, at that time I had no concept of apostolic ministry in a contemporary setting, and the church to which I belonged did not believe in it anyway. I was taught the Bible, but it was not until much later that I developed an understanding of the ministries and gifts of the Spirit, particularly the apostolic.

When I look back, however, I realize that even though I had a varied and exciting experience as a new Christian, the principal ministry then influencing me was that of teaching – a reformed evangelical expository preaching ministry on Sundays, a mid-week exposition and various different youth Bible studies. Like many other new believers, this period of my Christian life was wonderful and rich. I was learning a lot, but had no understanding of and little interest in church politics. I can remember scandalizing some of the older members by occasionally going along to a charismatic house church.

As the call to full-time Christian leadership began to emerge, the idea of being a 'missionary' began to be focused in a call and commitment to teach the word. I wanted to be a Bible teacher. So, at what now seems to be the ridiculously young age of 18, I went to theological college to train for ordination, and to prepare under the guidance of godly people for an expository ministry.

While I was at college, I came into contact with very gifted pastors who began to show me that teaching without pastoral care would achieve little, and both the care I received myself and the models of pastoral work that I was offered began to impress upon me the necessity of becoming a pastor as well as a teacher. Every so often I would remember the call to be a missionary and find myself confused about its fulfilment, since influences at theological college were equipping me for a different destiny.

I came to the end of my training somewhat disillusioned and confused about my future. I could not imagine how I could fulfil my 'missionary' call, given my discomfort with the roles that the more pastoral expressions of ordained ministry put on me. Rather than go forward for ordination, I decided to join a church team working in the inner city of London. I took up the task of face-to-face, front-line youth work. This was perhaps the first time that I was conscious of directly fulfilling the call to be a 'missionary'.

Without fully understanding it, I was helping to pioneer and plant a new work on the frontier. Seeing young people from the most disadvantaged backgrounds coming to know Christ began to fuel the fire of my calling again, and after two years I returned to theological training. Yet this only took me away from the frontier and began to frustrate me all over again. I was ordained at the age of 25. I had three theological degrees and a good deal of exposure to various kinds of ministry in different environments, but it seemed that I was no nearer to really knowing what I was about.

While I was serving my first year as a curate, I returned to my old university as part of a mission team led by the evangelist Eric Delve. I was profoundly impacted by the way in which God, by his Spirit, was able to convict people through Eric's dynamic presentation of the cross. Although I had seen many come to salvation, it had been largely through a relational method of evangelism or as a gradual 'dawning' of the call of Christ through a teaching ministry. Now I was presented with an evangelist whose gifts enabled him to call complete strangers to make a decision for Christ. I returned from the mission with a determination to emulate this kind of evangelism and to learn how to do it myself in a local situation. Maybe, if I was not a teacher or a pastor, I was an evangelist?

The only problem was that, try as I might, the fruit did not come. The special areas of responsibility that I had were producing little or no harvest. And although I was clever enough to present publicly an encouraging interpretation of what was happening, privately I was not clever enough to argue with my own secret fears. I had been ordained to a task that I could not achieve, and I feared that I was destined to live a life of relative failure.

I was finally brought to my knees through the accident mentioned in Chapter 3, which put me in hospital with serious burns to my legs that required extensive skin grafts. It was there, away from the influence of others, that God began to focus me in a direction that would ultimately release me into my calling. What happened as I lay in the isolation ward, unable to see or talk to anyone except the Lord, was that God got me to give up trying to live everyone else's dream and even the aspirations of my own dream, and to let him lead me in the direction of his choosing. I was utterly desperate and felt completely weak and so, when he spoke very clearly and told me to surrender to what it was that he wanted to do, I gave in and acquiesced to his desire. I was being drawn out of my comfort zone of familiar models of ministry into a frightening experience of always looking for the frontier of God's calling and the threshold of God's breakthrough.

I felt two kinds of pressure at the same time: the pressure to move ahead to find the frontier of the kingdom, and the pressure to wait for God's specific word before I stepped out. This was, in fact, a call to live on the boundary between excitement and fear – excitement at the prospect of God doing a new thing, and fear at stepping out before he directed. This tension soon became the defining context of my life.

While experiencing this tension, I also had an unmistakable confirmation of peace and a real feeling that this was what I was made for. As I attempted to plot this new course, the sense of rightness grew. Within a few months I began to see remarkable results. Literally dozens of young people were saved, people were healed and demons were cast out. These were the kinds of things I had always secretly wanted to happen, but I had come to believe that they were not for today, or that they were not for me.

I can remember identifying very much with Peter, whom I am sure felt this same strange cocktail of emotions when he stepped out of the boat to join Jesus on the water: an amazing rush of excitement at doing something which had never been done before (in itself a good description of a frontier); an awareness that what he was doing was impossible, and that if God did not do something special he was sure to drown. The tension between these two emotions was often a difficult balancing act. Sometimes one would emerge stronger than the other. Sometimes fear overtook excitement, and like Peter I began to look at the wind and the waves (see Matthew 14:30). At other times excitement so removed fear that I cast caution to the wind and attempted the craziest of things – just like Peter in the Garden of Gethsemane attempting to fight off the soldiers by cutting off Malchus's ear (see John 18:10). What was most important, however, was that I was beginning to learn how to function in my calling, and this brought the results for which I had always longed.

As this period of life and fruitfulness continued, I came into contact with those who could hear the Lord very clearly and I learned how to refine this gift in myself, spending many hours and much energy listening to and seeking to interpret God's prophetic words for the situations that I faced. A question emerged: maybe I was a prophet – one called by God to hear his word and articulate it to his people and the world? Certainly I had learnt to listen to his voice, but as I entertained this idea, I found myself moving from the epicentre of his blessing and striving to be something that was beyond me. With a growing sense that I was likely to burn out, I collapsed back into weakness and to letting God do whatever he wanted to do.

Almost immediately, the call to the frontier re-emerged. The strange combination of excitement and fear rose within me as God spoke to me about building a cross and carrying it round the parish that I now served in London, leading the church to the frontier with little more than faith to guard us. Again the fruit began to multiply and the blessings of God's Spirit began to flow back into my heart. All those years ago, God had called me to be a missionary and now here I was, using apparently foolish methods to find a way into the hearts of people who did not know God.

Interpretation

What happened over this fifteen-year period was that God defined my ministry by the effects of other ministries on my life. By a process of pressure and elimination, God showed me the meaning of my life's call: first I was equipped by the ministry of teaching, which called forth in me a desire to serve Christ in this way, then the pastors went to work on me and did the same thing, then the evangelists, and finally the prophets.

It is only now, as I see this process with the wisdom of hindsight, that I see that God's hand was working on me and pressing me into the inevitable conclusion: I was called to an apostolic ministry. Sometimes I ran out of grace to be one of the other ministries and crashed back to earth, having burned out in the attempt to be something I was never designed to be. Sometimes a sense of disillusionment with what it was that I was trying to do forced me to look elsewhere. One way or another, God used the experiences of life to push me finally into the ministry to which he had called me as a teenager.

I believe that many Christians find themselves in this same process, and what they do not realize is that God is working on them through the ministries of Christ to fashion them into the person he wants them to be. I think we have all found ourselves being challenged when we see God working powerfully through another person. Something in the way that God works through another attracts us and draws from us a desire to be able to function like them. I have heard of instances where this has happened and those who are drawn castigate themselves because they are desiring to be something that they are not and are therefore not content with what God has made them to be. Although godly contentment is a much prized virtue, however, I believe that part of God's intention is that, as he ministers to us through the channel of another, he draws us to desire to be that way ourselves. So God can use the evangelist to equip us to be more effective witnesses; the pastor to make us react with a greater compassion; the apostle to make us operate with greater authority. God does not want us to become something that we are not, but he does want to call forth in us a desire to be more complete in the calling that he has for us. As we become more mature, we learn to recognize the process of building and equipping and so are less likely to be pulled in different directions – 'blown here and there by every wind of teaching' (Ephesians 4:14) – but instead become rounded out, strengthened and matured in what we are called to be.

Uncertainty about what we should do arises out of a lack of security in who we are. This insecurity is built on unresolved questions of identity. In Ephesians, Paul goes to great lengths to define the general identity of Christians as being 'in Christ'. This is both settled and certain. By the time he arrives at the argument in chapter 4, he is able to refine this identity into the particular callings of the body of Christ. We have a double security, both general and particular. The general is eternally settled in the work of Christ; the particular is given to each Christian as a manifestation of the ministry of Christ here on earth. In this way, we all contribute to the strengthening and blessing of one another, and to the continuation of God's purposes among his people, so that as we express these ministries 'we will in all things grow up into him who is the Head . . . From him the whole body . . . grows and builds itself up in love, as each part does its work' (Ephesians 4:15–16).

In the rest of his letter, Paul goes on to describe how we should live and serve, but service is called forth from security and security is settled through the work of Christ on the cross once for all, and by the gifts of Christ through all, for all. In attempting to teach this, I have developed a vocabulary that I think begins to express what Paul is seeking to teach, and what Christ wants to release.

Base ministry

I believe that each of us has a base ministry that represents one of the five ministries of Christ spoken of in Ephesians 4. This ministry is our particular identity, part of God's design specification for our lives. As we come to Christ, this design spec has the potential to blossom into a tool of God's kingdom and an expression of Christ's life here on earth. Some people may identify with the rather prolonged and painful process of elimination that I went through, while others may not. Whichever it may be, we all need to have some tools that will enable us to identify the ministry to which we are called. In helping others to identify their base ministry, I have often begun with the idea of the pioneer–settler continuum. I have found that certain ministries are more 'pioneering' and others are more 'settling'. As we saw in the Reflections at the end of Chapter 3:

- A pioneer is someone who enjoys change and finds the stress of doing new things exciting rather than threatening. Pioneers are those who naturally reach out beyond their current experiences and relationships to discover new frontiers and challenges, and who find themselves frustrated by the disciplines needed to sustain what has already been established.
- Settlers have a great desire to grow what has been planted and develop what has been begun. There is a commitment to conserve, strengthen and 'flesh out' what has been initiated.

The church needs both the pioneers and the settlers. Without the pioneers, we would be less likely to reach out and find the new frontier, but without the settlers we would be unable to consolidate and keep what is won. Pioneers lead us into new things, but because they are always looking for 'the next new thing', we would probably lose as many frontiers as we gained. The settlers help us to hold the ground that we have already won, but because they are always looking to conserve and establish, they would probably over-elaborate and cease to reach out.

The pioneer ministries are the apostles, prophets and evangelists. The settler ministries are the pastors and teachers. As they interact with one another, they fashion the church into what God desires – a mature people of God. Interestingly, the interaction will create tension because the settlers will call the pioneers to consolidate, and the pioneers will challenge the settlers to move out from the familiar to the unknown. This tension, when unrecognized and unembraced, can cause the kinds of divisions and church splits that have often been part of the emergence of new movements within the church. The truth is that God has given the settlers to the pioneers to make them more whole, and vice versa. As we saw in the Reflection section of Chapter 3, it is part of God's strange economy that pioneers grow the most when they are forced to settle, and settlers grow the most when they are forced to reach out.

The pioneer–settler continuum is just one example of how God uses the ministries to interact with the others. As groups of ministries, the pioneers affect the settlers and vice versa, but of course the truth is that each individual ministry is also intended by God to have a profound effect on the others. In this way, each ministry becomes more rounded, of greater use to God and his people, and capable of achieving a greater impact and bearing more fruit.

If our base is pastoral, the other ministries will work on us to make us more complete and effective pastors. The teachers will call us to truth; the evangelists will challenge us to witness; the prophets will impress on us the need to listen to God; the apostles will motivate us to keep on the move. The pastors will learn that, although they may not be called to be teachers, they are called to speak the truth. They are not called to be prophets, and yet they are called to listen. They are not called to be evangelists, but they are called to witness. They are not called to be apostles, and yet they are called to go. The same rounding out, maturing and developing takes place with each person whatever their ministry: all the other ministries teach them how to be more complete and how to serve.

Phase ministry

All of this means that for each of us, as well as having a base ministry, we will find ourselves from time to time entering what I call a phase ministry – a time when we visit the environment of another anointing, not to stay, but only to sojourn. We are drawn there by the other ministries. By the teachers we are drawn into a phase of teaching; by the prophets into a time of the prophetic; by the evangelists into a period of evangelism; by the pastors into a time of caring for others; by the apostles into a period of striking out for the frontier.

If we are new to the process and unfamiliar with its pattern, we may believe that when this happens our ministry has changed, or that what has gone before was a mistake or a preliminary to what we now experience. Some will find themselves burning out as they run out of God's empowering grace to do a task for which he did not design them. Nonetheless, with good leadership and proper teaching, I believe that all can learn to identify the hand of God on their lives and the design and destiny that he has written for them.

Diagramatically, the process of base and phase ministries could be represented in the following way:

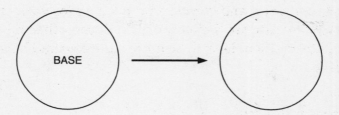

Another ministry influences us and draws us into a phase of learning to express the new and unfamiliar ministry.

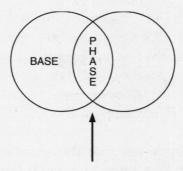

This leads us to enter a phase of new ministry. In time, with an exposure to all of the ministries, we are able to move from our base into new phases with ease. In fact, my observation is that those who have become mature in these things are able to move into a phase ministry without requiring the influence of the other ministries around them. Prompted by the Holy Spirit, or responding to what they see in their environment, they are able to operate with the effectiveness and freedom of all five ministries. Of course, however mature you are, you still have a base from which you minister most effectively, but now you are able to flow into any phase as the need arises.

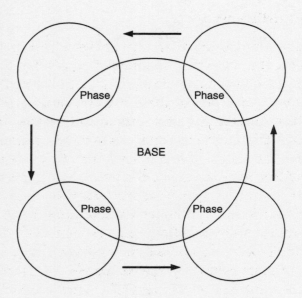

Some have suggested that the apostle has a special relationship to the other ministries and is therefore the primary ministry of the five. There is a suggestion that to be an apostle means to be able to function in all the other four ministries (this is sometimes pictured as the thumb of the hand being able to touch the other four fingers). Personally I find this suggestion slightly suspect, especially given that it is usually the apostles who teach it! My own view is that to be an effective apostle, mature in the calling of God as given, requires the ability to operate in all four other ministries as a phase. I also believe, however, that to be mature in any of the ministries requires the same thing.

Pre-Christian ministries

One of the interesting things that I have noticed, as I have followed through this interpretation of the text of Ephesians 4 and its application, is that God really has designed us for one of these five ministries. The pre-Christian counsellors and carers are pastors in the making; the educators and trainers are teachers in waiting; the salesmen and women are often evangelists just waiting to be saved; the creatives – artists, poets and writers – are pre-Christian prophets; the entrepreneurs are apostles in waiting. Although I would not want to press this argument too far, I find it interesting that Christians working in secular corporate environments are often recognized more readily by the companies for which they work than by the churches in which they serve.

Implementation

Of course, the proof of the pudding is in the eating, and for me this is the most exciting part. In the last chapter I mentioned the idea of two horizons – the first being a right interpretation of the text of Scripture, the second being an effective application in contemporary life. I also nailed my colours to the mast as far as my views on the interpretation of Ephesians 4 are concerned.

In this chapter, I would be so bold as to say that the implementation of the fivefold ministries (in terms of a base and phase ministry) has been the single most important teaching in the releasing of life through the many hundreds who have been gathered into the work of the church that I now serve.

Some would ask why it is that we do not have a greater emphasis on service rather than ministry, suggesting that it is more important that people develop a right kind of heart than understand who they are. To this I would reply that serving only ever comes out of identity. It was because Jesus knew he was the Son that he was prepared to sacrifice and serve. It is when we realize our identity as children of God that we are more released to serve the purposes of God, and it is when we know our place as children – i.e. know what our base ministry is – that we know how to serve and why to serve. God has given us the resources to be able to serve his purposes and to learn from others how that service might become more mature.

So I would say, with Paul, '[God has done this] to prepare God's people for works of service, so that [the people who make up] the body of Christ may be built up until we all reach unity in faith and in the knowledge of the Son of God and become [rounded, whole] mature, attaining to the whole measure of the fullness [comprehensive, complete and full expression of ministry] of Christ' (see Ephesians 4:12–13).

Reflections

Because my interpretation of Ephesians 4 and the five-fold ministry is not one with which people are very familiar, I am often asked questions that relate to the way this teaching works out in a person's ordinary, everyday experience. Here are just a few questions that are often asked, with particular reference (though not exclusively) to the apostolic ministry.

Do apostles always have 'out of the box' conversions?

Most people with an apostolic ministry never consider their conversion as anything out of the ordinary and yet often, if compared with the experience of many others, they have a peculiarity all of their own. For instance, not many with an apostolic ministry whom I have ever heard of or encountered experience a gradual thawing of their hearts. Instead they experience a definite moment when they meet God and hear his call. This encounter and call may not even be the first time that they are aware of God's presence, but there is an unmistakable quality to the experience which sets them apart and sends them out. As with the apostle Paul, there is a very clear sense of an encounter with God and a call that continues to resound throughout the person's life.

This may be because the apostolic ministry requires a great degree of individual perseverance and spiritual stamina. The call to the frontier is not a call to everyone, but requires a rugged determination that may find its origin both in the shaping of the personality and in the experience of conversion. Of course, there are many people who are not called into an apostolic ministry who have similar conversions or encounters with God, but in general I would say that the difficulty in fulfilling the commission is matched by the clarity of the call. For instance, it would take a lot for some people to hear God call them into full-time ministry in an established church, because the difficulty of remaining faithful and obedient within such a structure is so keen. It is often for these reasons that God gives a clear sense of call, so that when things get tough there is an unmistakable experience to which that individual can return.

How do you know what your base ministry is?

Your base ministry is the one that is the easiest for you to exercise – one that you have to put least effort into, one that in many ways seems just to happen all by itself. This is because grace has been provided to fit the shape of your personality in such a way that you naturally and instinctively fit the profile of this calling. Often it is difficult to recognize our own base, in the same way that it is difficult to describe our own nose or facial features. Our base ministry is so much part of us that we can miss it or become contemptuous of it because of our own familiarity.

Normal Christian experience will draw a person into various different experiences of phase ministry, and these will invariably end in struggle, difficulty, fruitlessness or burn-out. With time and maturity, we learn to recognize the boundaries of our grace within each phase and rest with the knowledge that we are still valuable to God, even though what we were most recently doing has now ceased to bear the marks of grace. Again with time, we become conscious of our place of rest and return – what we do when we stop doing everything else. This is the ministry which is easiest for us to exercise. Given humility and openness, this becomes our home – our base ministry.

How do you know when you are in a phase?

At first, a young or inexperienced Christian will often not know the difference between base and phase – everything is new, and it seems as though everything that is encountered is exciting and fresh. Over time, however, a person will begin to recognize the difference between grace that runs out because it is just the overlap of their base on other ministries, and grace that is more continuously available because it is the 'apportionment'.

For me, the easiest thing to do is to dream new dreams and start new projects. For someone who is not apostolic, this would not be their place of rest. It would not come naturally as their first spiritual instinct. When you have consciously gone through several cycles of phase ministry, it is possible to discern God calling you from a base into a particular phase. I am often conscious of God calling me into a season of teaching, specific pastoral care, prophetic or evangelistic ministry. I am sure that God's intention for each of us is that maturity (wholeness) leads to an ability and availability to move with freedom through all the ministries, moving from our base into the various phases.

One of the interesting things about base and phase is that it creates a clear overlap. For instance, a pastor may be called into an apostolic phase to pioneer a new pastoral practice, or an evangelist may be called into a prophetic phase to call the church to witness to a particular group of people.

Do apostles have to go through all the ministry phases?

The simple answer to this is 'no', but I believe that one definition of maturity is having been through all the phases and therefore being able to visit all of them again. For this reason I would always encourage leaders to be open to all the ministries, so that they can present a rounded leadership to the whole church. Such leaders would be more likely to be releasing and empowering of other people's ministries.

This is not an exhaustive list of questions, of course, and often one question leads to another. My encouragement is to heed the counsel of James: 'If any of you lacks wisdom, he should ask God, who gives generously to all without finding fault, and it will be given to him' (James 1:5).

9

Hinges of History

I am sure everybody remembers what they were doing on the 11th September 2001. I had just returned from a rather pleasant pub lunch with one of my local bishops when a member of my team told me the news. By the time I got home and turned on the 24-hour news channel, both towers of the World Trade Center had been hit and the screen was filled with replay images of the jetliners flying into those two huge buildings. Along with millions of others, I watched with growing horror as the WTC buildings burned and then collapsed into the streets of Manhattan. The images have etched an indelible mark on my memory, and surely the symbolism is lost on no one: before our eyes the icons of commerce and economic power crumbled. That night I called the celebration leaders of the church and asked them to contact their respective group leaders, who in turn would pass on to others my invitation to meet at the church to pray. With little more than an hour's notice, 300 people came. As a response to the unfolding situation, I read the passage I mentioned in Chapter 1, placing particular emphasis on the last two verses.

> At that time his voice shook the earth, but now he has promised, 'Once more I will shake not only the earth but also the heavens.' The words 'once more' indicate the removing of what can be shaken – that is, created things – so that what cannot be shaken may remain. Therefore, since we are receiving a kingdom that cannot be shaken, let us be thankful, and so worship God acceptably with reverence and awe, for our 'God is a consuming fire.' (Hebrews 12:26–9)

The whole world feels the aftershock of that day's momentous events. Few of us have what we could describe as an adequately worked out response to such things, but what is certain is that our world is now in the midst of tumultuous change, and the doors of history are beginning to swing on their hinges again.

In the wake of the World Trade Center tragedy, world leaders attempted a response. George W. Bush said his presidency had been defined by the events of the 11th September. His mission, and that of the nation he led, was now clear: to wage a 'war' on terrorism. The ideals of democracy and freedom were to be defended, and the free market – offering as it does the opportunities of development and prosperity for all – was to be protected. On the 11th September the USA was placed on a war footing, with both the Senate and House of Representatives (known for their cross-party rancour) offering an incredible level of unanimity in the cause.

The priorities of the richest and most powerful nation the world has ever seen have effectively been changed. Its history (some would add its destiny) and our whole world seem to have been altered for ever. Whether this proves to be true only time can tell – but this is what happens when the doors of history begin to swing: the hinges may be small, but the changes are vast.

God chooses to place the burden of history on the shoulders of mere men and women. People are the hinges. Swept up by events, they become the focus, the fulcrum, the point around which everything turns. Take George W. Bush, for example. By many estimates (including his own) he is not the most remarkable or gifted man to fill his office, and yet the events of history have ensured that his name will be remembered above and before many others who have stood in his position. Such are the days in which we live. God is looking for leaders who can become the hinges of history, those he can use to define the future.

The people God uses are not to be found in the expected places. Moses was taken from the bulrushes; David was found in the fields; Esther was found in the fashion parade. Like many others in the Bible, they were taken from obscurity into the centre of God's purposes. God consistently calls people from the edge into the centre, so that they in time can lead others from the centre to the edge.

Thus Peter was called from Galilee to Jerusalem, and was sent out from Jerusalem to the ends of the earth; Paul was called from the Damascus road to Antioch, and from Antioch to the world. And of course, when God chose to define this pattern (and to reveal what it means to be a hinge on which the doors of history hang), he sent his Son to be born in obscurity at the edge of an empire, so that he could journey to the centre of God's purposes and change the world for ever. If we are to be people given to such a purpose, it would be good to reflect more deeply on these things. To reflect means to answer the questions we pose ourselves.

- What are the similarities between this period of history and others when God has decisively intervened?
- What kind of person does God use to lead?

Perhaps in addressing these two questions we will begin to answer the challenges of our day.

1. What are the similarities between this period of history and others when God has decisively intervened?

In our opening chapter we began to explore these themes, but stayed very much with the contemporary culture. It is fascinating, however, to make reference to earlier times (both biblical and post-biblical) among the people of God, and compare them with today.

Moses

Moses was born into a world of massive insecurity. Unknown to those outside the corridors of power, the current ruling dynasty of Egypt was collapsing. The instruments of power and control had become over-stretched in a rapidly developing culture. The king and those in authority were intimidated by the presence of a numerous and rapidly multiplying alien people living among them. The Hebrews were no longer partners: they had become a threat. Insecurity inside and outside the kingdom led to pressure being focused on these foreigners, who could be used as the scapegoat for anxiety and the object of aggression. We all know the story.

First they were enslaved. Then they were overburdened. Finally, in exasperation, Pharaoh demanded the death of the firstborn sons, thereby limiting the ability of this now unwanted people group to reproduce. When civil authorities feel that they are out of control and that the events of a rapidly changing world are shaking them, they will often try to divert pressure away from themselves. Of course, when God begins to shake a nation, nothing can prevent the tide of change. In Moses' day, within a very short period of time a new dynasty and an even more developed, pyramid-building culture would emerge in Egypt. It was in this time of shaking that God chose to use Moses to liberate his people and fulfil his promise of a new future.

Moses was a man who was familiar with the world to which he was sent, compassionate towards those in need, and one who had been personally liberated by the desert experience. In him, God sent a person who was both competent and incompetent at the same time, both strong and weak, both powerful and humble. He drove him from the centre (the court of Pharaoh) to the edge (the far side of the desert) to lead his people on a journey through the desert to the Promised Land.

Today people are just as enslaved, but now it is to the

agendas of commercial success. They are just as over-burdened, but with the demands of contemporary life. Children have increasingly become an option rather than a necessity and are often presented as an obstacle to a happy and successful life. So first of all the population declines, and then abortion – the destruction of the future generation – is legitimized. Of course, the two cultures are quite different – there is little comparison between ancient Egypt and contemporary Western life – but in both contexts the shadowy figure of Satan stands ready behind the scenes, seeking to exert his evil power through the social structures that define the lives of God's people. And because his agenda remains unchanged, the effects on widely divergent cultures separated by distance and history are very much the same.

Will God choose to bring deliverance in our time, and offer again a new future only dreamed of by those enslaved?

David

The same pattern is repeated many times in the purposes of God. There was Joshua, and there were Judge-deliverers like Gideon and Deborah. Then there was David. He was the least of the least. He came from an unimportant family and an unimportant town. Socially, he was at the bottom of the pecking order – the eighth-born son, the one given the menial task of attending sheep. Yet it was from the fields that God brought him to the place of power. Even in his case, however, God did not use the most direct route. True to form, he first of all gave David great prominence and prestige by using him to kill Goliath. Then he allowed him to be driven from the court of King Saul into the Judean desert, the place David himself described as 'the ends of the earth' (Psalm 61:2).

It was a time of great anxiety and social upheaval: normal life was riven with the stress of wars and social strife. The economy was constantly overstretched. Conquest and famine lurked on the margins of everyone's life. People had to scramble just to scrape a living and keep their heads above water. Yet this was the time that God chose to raise up a great king who would lead the people into a time of unprecedented prosperity and peace.

Again, parts of our world, particularly the poorest, look very similar to the world of David's day. In the economically undeveloped parts of the world, life is ever in the balance and people feel constantly under threat. There is a tendency for the church to protect, hide, even run away. Could this be the time for God to raise up leaders of courage, 'hinges of history', who will carry the fight to the enemy and win the day?

Of course, we could also mention Esther, Ezra, Nehemiah and many others. All their stories – although unique in themselves – have a similar thrust and theme: God uses times of change, stress and even chaos to raise up leaders who will pioneer a new path to freedom.

Jesus and the apostles

In the New Testament we see the same trend. Jesus was born into a time of great change and social stress. Taxation was squeezing the life out of the people and society was becoming fissile and fractured, held to ransom by the competition between a superpower on the one hand and single-issue extremist groups on the other. This all sounds very contemporary, and yet this became the very balance point of history.

Peter, Paul and the other New Testament apostles present similar stories, all by now well known to us. After the close of the New Testament period, the desert fathers carried the torch of mission. Towards the end of this period, however, as Rome began to implode and the surrounding nations swept in from the unconquered regions, another great leader appeared on the scene.

Augustine had been educated in the centres of power, driven to the edge of despair by conviction of sin and the hopelessness of his spiritual condition, and brought to leadership of the church by the song of a child. 'Tolle, lege,' the child sang in the next-door garden. 'Take up and read.' Augustine picked up the scroll at his feet, the letter of Paul to the Romans, which he had been studying, and read:

> The night is nearly over; the day is almost here. So let us put aside the deeds of darkness and put on the armour of light. Let us behave decently, as in the daytime, not in orgies and drunkenness, not in sexual immorality and debauchery, not in dissension and jealousy. Rather, clothe yourselves with the Lord Jesus Christ, and do not think about how to gratify the desires of the sinful nature. (Romans 13:12–14)

So Augustine was converted. This scholar would be used by God to lead his people through the darkness towards the light. His leadership was not to be exerted in person, however, but through his writings. Those who had to navigate the darkened landscape of a world without Rome would rescue and pick up his scrolls. Augustine's theology and thought would form the foundation of the intellectual life of the known world for a thousand years.

After the collapse of the social framework that Rome had brought, and the emergence of the powerful, land-hungry Germanic tribes, the world was quite a different place. Whole people groups were on the move throughout Europe, and reaching them with the gospel became a task that presented a fresh challenge. To meet this need, the Celtic church was brought to prominence with its many great missionary leaders, such as Aidan, Brendan, Patrick, Columba and Brigid. Yet God's selection and training techniques were still the same – the methods of the New Testament.

These Celts were pilgrims on a missionary journey, which was taken in obedience to Christ. Their aim was both to follow him and to find him. The wanderings of the Celtic *peregrinati* took them all over Europe and beyond in the cause of Christ and his gospel. Their life and discipline informed the monastic movements of the Middle Ages and inspired such great figures as Francis of Assisi. In time, however, even this movement lost its fire and other leaders were then needed to lead the church in God's apostolic mission to the world.

Many others

There is no space to do more than mention Luther, the Augustinian monk who would rediscover the letter of

Romans, or Calvin, who framed again the doctrines of grace. We cannot explore the conversion of Wesley as he listened to the Moravian missionary Peter Bohler, read the introduction of Luther's commentary to Romans and found his heart 'strangely warmed'. What we can say, however, is that God has used these and many others in times of crisis and change to transform their spiritual landscape from the chaos of the world to that of the kingdom of his Son.

2. What kind of person does God use to lead?

It would appear that God chooses the gathering darkness to reveal the Light of the World, and the chaos of human striving to reveal the ordered peace of his kingdom. To do this, God needs leaders – leaders able to recognize the times, grasp the moment, and call people towards the future.

These leaders are the apostles of the new thing, those who define the future from the present. What kind of people are they?

They are called

Without a clear call, it is impossible to continue and press through when the challenges arrive. Trials and difficulties will certainly come, and a call will ensure that such times are not only met but won. Every person mentioned so far from the history of Scripture and the church had a clear and unmistakable sense of God's calling. God does not bargain or negotiate when he beckons, but commands. Recognizing this means that the person who is called knows that they are under

God's authority, and because they are under God's authority they will be much more able to exercise his authority.

They are clear

Vision is vital: it provides the purpose and momentum in leadership. Vision has two essential components. One is focused vision, the other is broad vision. The first grows as we respond to what God has said about the future. Our vision becomes our mission, and our mission is to extend the kingdom. Doing this will require clarity about what God has said and an ability to imagine creatively what such a future might hold. This vision will often be quite precise – planting a church, reaching a people group, impacting a city – and will draw us towards it and develop within us a determination to see it achieved.

The other form of vision, although closely related to the first, is one that enables us to step back from the narrow constraints of our preferred future and look at what God is doing in the present. Like Jesus, we have a joy set before us (a focused vision), but we also need to see what the Father is doing (develop a broad perspective). Without both of these elements of vision working together, problems will inevitably emerge. Leaders who are only able to see a vision of the future will tend to strive and drive others to see its fulfilment. This will lead to all kinds of stress and may produce burn-out, both in the leader and in the people who are led. On the other hand, a leader who only focuses on the present will be constantly reacting to the needs and conditions of those around him and will inevitably develop a work that lacks thrust and forward momentum.

Each of us is stronger in one of these dimensions of vision. For those who are strongest in focused vision, developing a breadth of perspective will mean that they are able to engage with the realities and difficulties of the present and bring much-needed grace and rest to the people they lead. Those who are strongest in having a broad perspective will benefit from developing their focused vision, because then they will be less likely to rush from one new thing to another, which in itself can become wearying. In doing so they will also develop a measured pace among the people they lead towards the future they desire.

When it comes to vision, clarity is the key.

They are confident

This is just another word for faith. It is absolutely essential, both for the spiritual health of the leader and for the work to be done. The Scriptures tell us that without faith no one can see God, and although this is most usually interpreted to refer to faith leading to salvation, it is also true of our life in general. We want to see the evidence of God's presence in all that we do, and especially in all that we lead. We want to see the evidence of God's presence in all that we plant and grow, and in the ministries and missions that we establish. We will see God when we have faith. Yet this confidence in God only emerges in one specific spiritual context: 'faith comes from hearing' (Romans 10:17). Notice that it does not say 'faith comes from reading, or from speaking'. There is a word that will come to us as we become familiar with the Scriptures and the ways of God. This is the word spoken directly to us by Christ. Such a word is heard within us, and is recognizable because it creates faith. Without this, it is almost impossible to carry the challenge of apostolic leadership and the costs that it brings. It is closely related to call and clarity of vision, but it is a more routine experience. With immersion in the Scriptures and maturity in discipleship, it becomes a regular feature of our daily walk.

They are courageous

This is, of course, closely related to confidence and to the other components of character mentioned above. Together, call, clarity and confidence lead to a courageous commitment to engage the enemy in his own territory and to win the day by leading God's people to extend the frontiers of his kingdom. In times of difficulty and crisis, courage will define those who become victors from those who become victims. It will mark the difference between those who change the world for good and those who do not. Leaders need courage. Without it they cannot possibly take on the task to which they are called.

Courage is not bravado or human endeavour. It is the fruit of one who is called by God, clear about their vision, confident in their faith, and prepared to pay the cost. All of these are vital components in the character of an effective apostolic leader, and when held together in God's hand and fashioned into a life of obedience, they become something powerful to the purposes of God. What do they produce? They produce a person who is a pioneer, planter, bridger and builder.

It may be that the apostolic is your lifelong calling

and your base ministry. It can also be a temporary calling, however; a phase ministry to which you are called for a time in order to see a breakthrough within the work to which you are called and among the people with whom you are called to work.

You may remember that *pioneers*:

- claim lives as new territory for the kingdom of God;
- proclaim the gospel to any who will hear;
- act decisively with enemy counterattacks;
- operate in divine authority and power;
- establish bridgeheads from which they can work.

Extending the frontier in this way will mean that the pioneers will also be able to become *planters*, who:

- recognize the right time to plant;
- identify the people who can open doors to other relationships;
- prioritize relationships over popularity;
- focus their energies and gifts into small, gathered groups;
- impart patterns of community life that can grow and multiply.

Sometimes pioneering and planting will require us to step out of our familiar environment and culture and so become *bridgers*, who:

- recognize the different needs of different cultures;
- communicate appropriately according to cultural needs;

- use their pioneering and planting gifts to establish cross-cultural bridgeheads;
- address cultural prejudices among disciples so that their eyes are opened to the new bridging opportunities.

Whether we bridge into new cultures or not, pioneering and planting will require that we develop lightweight strategies and low-maintenance structures so that the work can be sustained. In other words, we will become *builders*, who:

- develop teamwork;
- commit to a shared life;
- share common resources;
- produce repeatable teaching;
- create strategies for mission.

Whether we are lifelong apostles or in an 'apostling' phase, we will to some extent reflect these components in our ministry.

Missionary journeys from the centre to the edge

For me, an apostolic calling has meant a series of journeys, but each of these journeys, whether real or metaphorical, has displayed the same characteristics and has produced a similar result. Christ has beckoned me to leave the comfort and familiarity of an institutionalized faith, with its 'corporate' mentality and 'company' feel. The old ways, words and worship, though rich in history and redolent of past victories, no longer work.

There are new ways and words which express the unchanging truth for a new world. There are new ways to worship 'in spirit and in truth' (John 4:24).

This journey has often carried me to the margins of the denomination in which I have been called to serve, and although I have remained loyal, it has placed me in an uncomfortable and prophetic position on the edge of the institution. Here, however, I have found the kingdom's frontier; here I have found Jesus the apostle calling me into his mission; and here I have found the fruitfulness for which I have longed. Nonetheless, with the fruitfulness and success has come a temptation and a potential trap. I now sit at the centre of a large and growing church, and could easily become remote from the people I am called to lead in mission. I have no direct involvement in, and sometimes little knowledge of, most of what happens across the life of the church that I lead.

I hear other apostolic figures tell me that this is the destination of all who are apostolic, to exercise leadership and authority from the midst of God's people. I see others eager to embrace this status and this role. Yet I also hear another voice, barely audible over the tumult of success – the voice of Christ himself calling me on. 'Come to the boundary, follow me to the edge, lead others to the frontier.' And so I am committed to another journey – a missionary journey from the centre to the edge, from the centre to the place where Jesus wants to pioneer a new work, plant a new thing, bridge and build into new communities.

As with the Celtic saints, I find myself called in this way to fulfil the mission of Christ. I must ever seek and find the frontier of God's purposes. What I discover

each time on this journey is that Christ has prepar[
way. Already there are others in place; often the people
of the church have made the journey themselves. I, the
leader, find myself in an odd way having to follow, but
getting there second does not mean that you are not
still called to lead. Someone has to shape, structure and
strategize for the breakthrough to be made. I have often
seen godly believers waiting on the margins for their
leaders simply to come and lead. Some have given up,
made weary by the waiting. If we are called to lead, we
must make the journey. And if we make the journey, we
will find that the Lord will keep his promise and supply
our needs.

The challenge of the day

For those of us who live in the West, the task is to escape
the shackles of institutional Christianity and engage
with the cultural captivity of those whom we meet in
the world. Like Moses and all those pioneering leaders
who followed him in the Old and New Testaments, and
throughout the history of the church, God is preparing
us for a great new work. As God strips away the self-
reliance of the mainstream denominations and takes us
into the desert of dependency on him, we will – like
Moses – find ourselves being led to the mountain of
meeting where God will cause his fire to fall, fire that
frees us so that we in turn become the liberators that
God needs to meet this hour. The world around us is
captive, but the church is equally enslaved. God needs
leaders who can set his people free to reach a lost and
darkened world.

These are the questions for those who lead the church in apostolic mission:

- Are we ready to go?
- Are we prepared to be 'sent out' into such a world of flux and change?
- Are we clear about the message we proclaim?
- Are we confident in the methods we use?

When Jesus called his first apostles, his desire was 'that they might be with him and that he might send them out to preach' (Mark 3:14). Knowing that Jesus wants us with him and that this is the desire of his heart gives us all the confidence we need. Confidence to go out is based on knowing that we always return to him.

We also know, however, that the task of one who is 'sent out' is to proclaim, and in proclaiming to pioneer and plant, bridge and build. We are sent out by one who loves us to a world for which he died, to present a life-transforming message in terms that can be understood. The message has not and must not be changed, but the language used to convey the truth should always be adapted to the new place and culture to which we are sent.

We see the dawning of a new day, but we see it only with the eyes of faith – for, as so often, the hours before dawn are the darkest.

When George VI was looking for words that would capture the moment and prepare his people to face the struggle of a world at war, he found these sentiments to share in his Christmas broadcast to the nation in 1939:

A new year is at hand. We cannot tell what it will bring. If it brings peace, how thankful we shall all be. If it brings us continued struggle, we shall remain undaunted. In the meantime, I feel that we may all find encouragement in the lines which in my closing words I would like to say to you all:

'I said to the man who stood at the gate of the year, "Give me a light that I may tread safely into the unknown." And he replied, "Go out into the darkness and put your hand into the hand of God. That shall be to you better than light and safer than a known way." '[1]

Surely this is the call of our day. We need leaders who are able to echo and live out such statements of courage and commitment. Although the church's position of power has been lost and our numbers have greatly declined, all is not lost. We have one who can lead us, and he looks for those whom he can use to lead.

Personal response

On several occasions I have found myself as a church leader challenged to make the journey from the centre to the edge. In these last few years, God has called me to connect specifically with those in my own church who work among the poorest of our contacts, not only so that the people called to this ministry will feel connected with all that the church is doing, but also so that I can be personally grounded in the most volatile of the frontiers we are seeking to extend. As our church has gone through its own experience of 'concentration

---

[1] From a poem called 'God Knows' written by Miss Minnie Louise Haskins, a lecturer at the London School of Economics.

and spread',[2] however, I have been called to take missionary journeys to the places where our small church plants (which we call clusters) are being established.

Several years ago the Lord led us to move a large portion of our congregation into the city centre. This led to even larger numbers of people being gathered to two large celebrations. In time, God began to prepare us for the spreading out of the clusters that made up these larger city-centre gatherings. First, God sent us prophetic leaders who spoke of God 'stirring up the nest' like the eagle in Deuteronomy 32, and then there came a strong impression within me that the time of this stirring and dispersal was getting closer. We spent over a year ensuring that the structures of support and oversight were properly in place, and then God moved. Although we had plenty of warning and time for preparation, the end seemed very sudden. God saw to it that our large city-centre facility was closed on safety grounds and made unavailable to us because its owners were now seeking to sell it on – but not to us.

As I write today, St Thomas's is dispersed throughout the city in many missional communities – sixteen of which were sent out in one Sunday. We gather all of these together monthly in a large rented facility for worship, teaching and encouragement. If anyone had told me when I was ordained that this was what I would be doing in the future, I am sure I would have run a mile!

---

[2] Bob Hopkins and Richard White, *Enabling Church Planting* (CPAS, 1995), p. 5.

Reflections

A vision for winning a city

In October 1990, God gave me a very clear vision in which I saw a battle unfold before my eyes. As it did, God interpreted to me a strategy for mobilizing the church to win neighbourhoods and cities. It seemed to me that God was saying that the devil was prepared to surrender as many individual converts as it took to keep the churches comfortable in their vision for church growth, as long as this prevented them from setting their eyes on impacting a whole city. In November and December of that same year, I taught this strategy to the church I then led in Brixton, London – but imagine my surprise when, only a few months later, I saw the whole vision played out on our television screens. Since then I have carried it with me as a prophetic picture of what God seeks to do in and through us.

On the 16th January 1991 the Allied forces present in the Gulf launched one of the greatest bombardments in any battle of the twentieth century. Under the leadership of General Colin Powell and General Norman Schwartzkopf, the American and Allied forces unleashed a barrage of the most powerful conventional weapons known to man. The battle began with a bombardment from the air, followed by artillery from the ground and the sea. This destroyed the Iraqi communication network and rendered its air force and armoured units almost completely ineffective.

Having softened up their targets in this way for a number of weeks, the Allied mobile armoured units were readied to move against the enemy lines. The divisions of marine and tank regiments broke through on the first night. The Iraqis were completely surprised and outflanked by their aggression and speed. Once the breech had been made, the ground troops and infantry divisions were able to move in and take up positions in enemy territory. These ground troops and others that followed then gathered the captives, took part in mopping-up operations and finished off any remaining pockets of resistance.

The entire operation, including the air, sea and land offensive, took only a few weeks to complete. The ground battle itself took only a few days. The victory was possibly the most comprehensive military achievement of the twentieth century.

Paul was familiar with the military metaphor, which from time to time he developed in his writings. The best known example, of course, is Ephesians 6:10–20, where he articulates his understanding of spiritual warfare and our need for the armour of God. I am sure that if Paul were around today he would be open to the same kind of metaphor, drawn from contemporary military campaigns.

Even if I had not had the vision, I think I would have felt that Desert Storm was significant, because it has the potential to be developed into a comprehensive strategy to win the communities to which we are sent. But how?

1. Desert Shield

Even before the forces began to gather in Saudi Arabia, 'special forces' units of British and American troops were dropped behind enemy lines into the desert. Some disguised themselves as Bedouins, and began gathering information and intelligence about the enemy's strength and movements. When the air offensive had begun, these spies on the ground provided invaluable information on the effectiveness of the Allied bombing campaign and helped target the Allied ordinance.

While this 'secret war' for intelligence was being waged, other things were being prepared by the Allied and American troops. Before a single shot was fired, or one prisoner taken, marines and others built the camps that would hold all the prisoners of war, the kitchens that would feed the troops and the hospitals that would take care of the wounded.

The first stage had two parts – one that used special forces behind the enemy lines, and another that developed an infrastructure which was able to support the war effort and deal with the effects of victory.

2. Desert Storm

(a) This stage was the struggle for dominance in the air. It focused on breaking up the enemy's lines of communication and ability to respond to attack. Once air superiority was established, the ground troops could move into place. Without this, the infantry and armoured units would have been severely compromised and exposed.

(b) The bombardment of the enemy lines intensified when the air campaign was supplemented by an artillery barrage. The principal aim of this new phase in the battle was to 'soften' the enemy's front line and create the possibility of a breakthrough. Of course, both aircraft and artillery were also used at later stages to support the ground war. Artillery backup and 'close air support' are still familiar features of modern warfare.

(c) Stage three dealt with the mobilization of ground troops. Tanks and fast-moving infantry units travelling in armoured personnel carriers transported the troops to, and through, the opposing lines. Some were delivered by helicopter; others were dropped by parachute directly into the theatre of operations to deploy forces on the ground more rapidly. The intention was to break through, take ground and render the enemy incapable of fighting back.

(d) The final part of the battle was that of mopping up and gathering the captives. The camps built before the military campaign began now came into their own. Few can forget the images of Iraqi soldiers begging American marines to take them prisoner. All their morale and the bravado of their leaders had gone. All they wanted was to surrender and for the fighting to stop.

Interpretation

1. Desert Shield

The 'secret war' of intelligence-gathering and targeting is similar to the prophetic tasks of intercession and cultural interpretation. Intercession, when mobilized across the whole church, becomes the battle for the air. It forces the enemy into a corner and causes him to run for cover. As long as prayer and intercession are going up, the enemy's ability to move and fight back is severely limited. A burden for intercession must be birthed in the church so that God can release the battle in the air. The church needs intercessors as much as Desert Storm needed aeroplanes. This intercession must be informed, however. We must understand the communities in which we live and the culture with which we are called to engage. Only then will we begin to recognize where the enemy is hiding and how our prayers should be directed.

In the same way, we need to develop infrastructure as part of our preparation for mobilization and growth in the church. Wisdom dictates that we should develop an internal structure to the church which is both flexible and sustainable. Something along the lines of cells, congregations and celebrations will almost certainly be needed if a church is to sustain continuous and significant growth.

When this preparation has been done thoroughly, these differently sized church groups become places where newly converted 'prisoners of grace' are gathered. Programmes become a way of catering for the feeding and healing of the 'soldiers'. These will range from developing ministry teams through to evangelistic and training courses such as Alpha.

2. Desert Storm

For the battle in our cities to be successful, we need to gather, train and equip apostolic teams to move into the neighbourhoods, communities and people groups to which we are called. This will require a release of the apostolic characteristics of pioneering, planting, bridging and building. If the preparation in stage one has been a success, then the campaign on the ground can be led by the apostles. Here we find an overlap between Desert Shield and Desert Storm – a close interaction between the prophetic and the apostolic. The function of the prophetic is to develop insight and intercession, and the function of the apostolic is to develop infrastructure and strategy.

The importance of unity

The victory of Desert Storm was provided by the preparation of Desert Shield. Unified under the umbrella of the United Nations and the leadership of the United States, many nations including Britain came together as a single force in the Gulf. This to me is a sign of the need for unity in our church, and across the churches, for victory to be assured.

The importance of all the ministries

A strategy of this kind is only successful if all five of the ministries and the whole body of Christ are mobilized. We need the prophets to instruct the church with the insights necessary for effective prayer. We need the apostles to define the structures and strategies and to lead the spearhead of mission. We need the evangelists to gather up the newly released 'prisoners of grace'. We need the teachers to feed the troops. We need the pastors to head up the hospital work of caring and healing.

The mission is to win

Carrying the mission of God into the world will meet resistance, both seen and unseen, but undoubtedly the

unseen foe represents the most powerful and dangerous opponent. The mission is to 'go into all the world',
but to do that we must be committed to paying the sacrificial price of lives 'laid down' to win the victory.

APPENDIX

Fivefold Ministries
– Results of Questionnaire

From p. 171, working from left to right, transfer the grand totals shown on that page to the boxes below to discover your base and phase ministries (see p. 161).

Grand total   Grand total   Grand total   Grand total   Grand total

☐   ☐   ☐   ☐   ☐

PASTOR   PROPHET   TEACHER   EVANGELIST   APOSTLE

The Prophet's Notebook

by Barry Kissell

Today God is restoring the prophetic ministry to his church. There is a lively interest in the gift of prophecy today. But what does it mean to live and function in the prophetic? Barry Kissell shares openly his experiences, joys and tribulations in the school of the prophet. He writes for both those who share his calling and for those who wish to explore.

'In this notebook I have tried to be as frank and honest as I can be. I have shared revelations that have, over the years, proved to be of God, but I have also covered the unfulfilled and the unknown . . . My prayer for you is that you will take this calling seriously and will begin the great journey of seeking to know God and to hear his word.' (Barry Kissell)

BARRY KISSELL is married to Mary and they have seven children. For 29 years he was a leader at St Andrew's Chorleywood and is now Associate Vicar at St Mary's, Bryanston Square, London. For 25 years he had an itinerant ministry which took him with Faith Sharing Teams to hundreds of churches in the UK and to 25 nations.

MINISTRY GUIDES

The Evangelist's Notebook

by John Peters

John Peters believes we need to make radical changes in the way we evangelise. Why would non-Christians want to come to church if they can't understand what's going on and if we are unable to explain to them, in everyday language, exactly what we believe?

The author looks at what it takes to be an evangelist and shares his own experiences. He urges us to concentrate on the essential truths in our evangelism and to be open to the Spirit's leading in our conversations with unbelievers.

JOHN PETERS is an ordained Anglican minister and is currently the leader of St Mary's, Bryanston Square. He lives in central London with his wife Jenny and their three children.

MINISTRY GUIDES

The Reluctant Exorcist

by Ken Gardiner

Ken Gardiner draws on his personal experience and true stories, acquired during 30 years of ministry, to provide guidelines to anyone who feels they should know more about deliverance and related ministries. With common sense and spiritual wisdom he examines such issues as

- distinguishing between mental disorder and demonisation
- possession versus oppression
- how evil spirits can gain access to individuals, including believers
- the cleansing of places
- involvement in the occult, and psychic abilities
- paranormal phenomena, including ghosts and poltergeists
- who or what are demons?

CANON KEN GARDINER has ministered in the area of deliverance for over 30 years. Now retired, he lives in Rochester and still serves on the deliverance ministry advisory board of his local diocese.

MINISTRY GUIDES